BODY LIFE

Discovery House Publishers

Books, music, and videos that feed the soul with the Word of God

Box 3566 Grand Rapids, MI 49501

BODY LIFE

Revised and Expanded
by James D. Denney

RAY C. STEDMAN

Body Life
Copyright © 1972 by Ray C. Stedman
Revised Edition Copyright © 1995 by Elaine Stedman

Discovery House Publishers is affiliated with RBC Ministries,
Grand Rapids, Michigan 49512

Discovery House books are distributed to the trade exclusively by
Barbour Publishing, Inc., Uhrichsville, Ohio 44683

Unless indicated otherwise, Scripture quotations are from *The
Revised Standard Version of the Bible.* Copyright © 1946 and 1952 by
the Division of Christian Education of the National Council of the
Churches of Christ in the United States of America. Used by
permission.

Library of Congress Cataloging-in-Publication Data

Stedman, Ray C.
        Body life / Ray C. Stedman.
                p.   cm.
        ISBN 1-57293-000-4
        1. Church. 2. Church renewal. 3. Christian life. I. Title.
BV600.2.S75   1995
262—dc20   95-21478
                                                                CIP

Printed in the United States of America

02 03 04 05 06 / CHG / 10 9 8 7 6 5 4 3

CONTENTS

Foreword by Billy Graham   7

Publisher's Preface to the Revised Edition   9

Chapter 1:   The Most Powerful Force on Earth   11

Chapter 2:   The Church's Highest Priority   21

Chapter 3:   Not Union—Unity   39

Chapter 4:   All God's Children Have Gifts   59

Chapter 5:   Discovering and Using Your Gift   77

Chapter 6:   According to the Power   87

Chapter 7:   How the Body Works   99

Chapter 8:   Shaping Up the Saints   119

Chapter 9:   The Work of the Ministry   133

Chapter 10:   Keeping the Body Healthy   149

Chapter 11:   The Goal Is Maturity   165

Chapter 12:   Impact!   193

Body Life Problems and Solutions   219

Study Guide   225

Notes   267

FOREWORD

to the original edition of

Body Life

Much is being said today about the church being irrelevant. With many observers of the religious scene, the church has become the whipping boy for many of the world's ills.

It depends, of course, on how one defines the "church." In *Body Life*, Ray C. Stedman uses the leverage of the Word itself to bring us back to the church's real meaning and mission. With strong, convincing argument he points to the weaknesses within the institutional church, and clearly reminds us of the strength inherent in Christ's body, the *true* church.

This book is not all theory and semantics. In chapter 12, the author relates how his interpretation of the church has worked effectively in the crucible of practical experience. He convinces us that the New Testament definition of the church is the outworking of Christ Jesus through His corporate body.

His Peninsula Bible Church (PBC) began with only five laymen who felt the need for more meaningful and effective Christian witness, and a richer *koinonia*-fellowship than they were accustomed to. These five, convinced that the church too often boxed itself behind stone walls, took the church to the people of their community with sincerity, dedication, and effectiveness. Today, it is one of the most dynamic companies of Christian believers on the West Coast.

Ray C. Stedman, eager to share PBC's blessings with other groups, has given us a "how-to" book which shows us how the church can relate to community life in a meaningful, satisfactory, and redeeming manner.

Billy Graham

PUBLISHER'S PREFACE

to the Revised Edition

A generation has gone by and the world has changed tremendously since the original edition of *Body Life* was first published in 1972. The concepts of *Body Life* were hammered out during the spiritual and cultural ferment of the era of Vietnam, the Great Society, the Apollo space program, Haight-Ashbury, and Watergate—and these concepts have stood the test of time.

The core principles of *Body Life* are as true today as they were in the '60s and '70s. Why? Because they didn't originate in that era. They originated in the same place that Christianity itself originated—in the mind of God, the heart of God, and the Word of God.

This book, Dr. Stedman's masterpiece on the nature and function of authentic Christianity, has always been a readable and practical favorite. This new edition, however, has been completely revised to make it even *more* readable, *more* user-friendly, *more* applicable to the world in which we live—the world at the beginning of the twenty-first century. A study guide has also been added at the end of the book to help make the concepts of *Body Life* real in your own life and the life of your church.

This book served as a blueprint for a spiritual revolution in the 1970s. Now, a generation later, its truths are even more timely and practical than ever before. We stand at the brink of a new millennium, facing a brave new world of cyberspace and virtual reality, AIDS and widespread moral breakdown, new genetic technologies, new weapons technologies, spiraling crime rates, racial warfare, and societal decay. The need has never been greater for the church to be re-energized and re-dedicated to its original purpose.

The church *must* become the church God intended it to be. We *must* become the kind of Christians God intended us to be. We *must* learn again to practice deep *koinonia*-fellowship, carrying one another's burdens, sharing one another's hurts, confessing to one another, rejoicing with one another, encouraging one another, celebrating the diversity of our gifts and abilities while maintaining the unity of the Spirit.

As our world rolls into the twenty-first century and the third millennium, we *must* rediscover the meaning of *Body Life*—the amazing energy and empowerment God gives to His people when they live in close, loving, caring community with Him and with one another. So we commend to you, as a committed follower of Christ, this new edition of a genuine Christian classic—a book not only to read, but to implement, to live in, to build upon.

It will change your church. It will change your life. Welcome to the adventure of *Body Life!*

CHAPTER 1

THE MOST POWERFUL FORCE ON EARTH

This book is about the church.

Not the church as it often is, but the church as it originally was. The church as it can be. And yes, the church as it *must* be again.

What sort of image does the word *church* bring to your mind? Does it suggest to you—

• A snooty religious country club, bound by strange, almost secret rituals, traditions, and jargon?

• A political action group, waging war on behalf of a social agenda (of either the left or the right)?

• A waiting room, where people wait expectantly but rather passively for the next bus to heaven?

• A collection of hypocrites who care more about expensive pipe organs, stained glass, and stone buildings than they do about the hurting and hungry in the world?

• A place where religious junkies gather to get their "feel-good fix" so they can get through another week?

• A collection of sanctimonious killjoys who want to legislate morality for the rest of the world?

Let's be honest: The church has been *all* of these things at one time or another. Again and again, it has justified every bitter charge, every gripe and criticism that was ever leveled against it by angry atheists and disillusioned agnostics.

Yet—despite all its obvious flaws, weaknesses, hypocrisies, sins, and excesses—the church has been the most powerful force for good on the face of the earth, century after century, from the time of the apostles right up to this present moment. It has been light in the midst of the blackest darkness. It has been salt—both a preservative and a delightful seasoning—in a corruption-prone, unsavory society.

A paradox? Absolutely! Many of the most wonderful truths of God come packaged in a paradox, wrapped in a mystery. As we unravel the seeming contradictions of God's church—as He designed it and created it to be—we will find some of the deepest, most exhilarating, and life-changing of all of God's truths.

The truths of *Body Life*.

Two churches

How can we unravel this paradox? How can the church be both sin-ridden *and* salt and light? How can the church be both a source of disillusionment and a source of illumination at the same time? The answer, as found in the Bible, is this: What we call "the church" is really *two* churches! One is selfish, power-hungry, and sinful. The other is loving, forgiving, and godly. One has a long history of stirring up hatred, conflict, and bloody persecution, all in the name of God and religion. The other has always sought to heal human hurts, break down barriers of race and class, and deliver men and women from their guilt, shame, fear, and ignorance.

One is a *false* church, a counterfeit, masquerading as Christianity, but whose head is Satan. The other is the *true* church, founded by Jesus Christ, mirroring His authentic character through acts of love, self-sacrifice, courage, and truth.

For some reason, we are continually surprised when we are confronted by this counterfeit church. For some of us, a painful encounter with this false church creates so much pain and disillusionment that we actually begin to doubt the reality of God and His true church! But we shouldn't be surprised or disillusioned when we bump up against counterfeit Christianity. Jesus Himself predicted that the false church would come.

In Matthew 13, Jesus uses a series of parables (that is, allegorical stories) to describe conditions in the world during the interval between His first coming and His second coming. That interval is the age in which we now live, and one of the parables He told is called the parable of the wheat and the tares. Another word for *tares* is *weeds*. In this story, Jesus says that He Himself, as the Son of Man, plants wheat in the field of the world. The wheat, He says, represents Christians, whom He calls "the sons of the kingdom."

But after the wheat is planted, the devil comes in and plants weeds. These weeds, or tares, look like wheat but produce no grain. The tares are, in effect, false or counterfeit wheat. These tares represent false or counterfeit Christians, whom Jesus calls "sons of the evil one." Outwardly, these false Christians look like the genuine article, just as the tares look like real wheat. The wheat and tares grow up together, and are completely indistinguishable from each other—for a while.

Soon, workers notice the weeds growing among the wheat and come asking if they should dig up the weeds. The Lord's answer: *Absolutely not!* Uprooting the tares would destroy the wheat along with the weeds. Instead, "let both grow together until the harvest" (Matthew 13:30).

The harvest, Jesus concludes, will take place at the close of the age when He sends His angels (not men) into the field to separate the weeds from the wheat. The weeds will be burned in judgment, but the wheat will be gathered into His father's barns. The wheat—the true Christians, the sons of the kingdom—are those who have experienced what the Bible calls the new birth. As Jesus says in another passage, "Unless one is born anew, he cannot see the kingdom of God" (John 3:3).

The apostle Peter later describes the genuine Christians as being "born anew, not of perishable seed but of imperishable, through the living and abiding word of God" (1 Peter 1:23). The sons of the evil one are the false Christians, never born again by the power of the Spirit of God through faith in the Word of God, but who purport to be Christians because:

- They have fulfilled some outward religious ritual;
- They have joined a local church;
- They are relying on outward moral conduct; or
- They want to cloak their own evil and sin in an outward covering of religiousness.

In the sight of God, they are children of Satan. To other people, and even to themselves, they are indistinguishable from the true Christians.

No wonder the church presents such a confused picture to the world! If we ignore the biblical picture, as illustrated by the parable of the wheat and the tares, then the church appears confusing even to those who love and defend it!

If we are unable to recognize the dual, "true-and-false" nature of the church, if we insist on viewing these two distinct churches as one and the same, then we are doomed to a kind of "ecclesiastical schizophrenia" that will leave us baffled and confused.

"But," you may ask, "isn't there *any* way we can separate the true church from the false?" It has been tried many times before, and every such attempt has failed because the separation has been attempted on the basis of external factors: doctrinal purity, moral conduct, ritualistic practices, and even affiliation with the government! Roman Catholics have insisted they have the true church. Baptists have scorned such claims and declared that they have the true pattern. Other sects and denominations have arisen and declared, "A plague on both your houses—*we* are the true church!" And so the battle has raged for centuries.

The result of all this confusion and bickering has been that the church has increasingly been robbed of its sense of identity. Like someone suffering from amnesia, the church is asking, "Who am I and what am I here for?"

Two-in-one Christians

The truth is, of course, that *no* religious organization or denomination can be the true church. The division between true church and counterfeit church does not lie along denominational lines. True Christianity is not a matter of organizations or groups.

"Well, then," you might say, "it must be an individual matter. What we have to do is examine the lives of individual Christians. Those who manifest counterfeit Christianity are counterfeit Christians. Those who manifest true Christianity are true Christians."

If only it were that simple! According to the Bible, however, it's a lot more complicated than that. It's true that, biblically, counterfeit Christians can only manifest counterfeit Christianity. However, *true* Christians are capable of displaying *both* true and false Christianity—though not at the same time. Genuine Christians can, through ignorance or willful disobedience, display a false and counterfeit Christianity in their lives. When they do, they cause as much harm as the irreligious, self-centered pagans around them! They bring the gospel into disrepute, and they bring shame and dishonor to their Lord.

The sad truth is that it is deceptively easy to be a Christian yet not live a Christian life. Even though living in disobedience is dull, barren, and deadly, and even though the true Christian life is vital, exciting, and effective, many Christians choose disobedience. They bring hurt to themselves and the people around them—and they grieve the heart of Jesus.

As we enter a new millennium, the great masses of

people across this world are confused and afraid. They are searching for reality. They are desperate for a place of safety in a world beset with terrorism, rampant crime, racial unrest, AIDS, the threat of nuclear and biological warfare, the threat to the environment, and more. Today's headlines seem to be moving us toward the last days foretold by Jesus, Daniel, and John's Revelation—and toward the harvest of the wheat and the tares.

So it is all the more urgent today that we search out from Scripture the true nature and function of authentic Christianity, and that we recover the dynamic energy and power of the early church. As we cross the threshold of the twenty-first century, the world seems to be a terribly complicated place— especially when compared with the world of the early church. And yet, there is no reason why the church in the twenty-first century should not be what it was in the first century. True Christianity operates on exactly the same basis now as it did then. The same power that turned the world upside-down in the book of Acts is available to us today.

What keeps us from experiencing that power today? I believe the major barrier we face is *ignorance.* Most Christians are tragically unaware of the biblical pattern for the church. Even true Christians, the true wheat, still vainly attempt to do what their Master told them was hopeless and counterproductive: to physically separate the wheat from the weeds (see Matthew 13:24–30). We need to realize that elements of true and false Christianity will be intermingled in the same world, in the same church, even in the same person. Any attempt to weed out the false runs the risk of uprooting the true as well. Our goal as Christians should not be to go on a search-and-destroy mission against all the tares in the church, but to do everything we can to make the true wheat in the church so strong and healthy that the tares are powerless to damage it.

Jesus declared that He would build His church upon a rock, an unshakable foundation. That rock was the fact of His Messiahship and deity, as the apostle Peter confessed (see Matthew 16:16). Subsequently, on the day of Pentecost, His church came into being by the power of the Spirit of God. At first there was no sign of the presence of false Christianity. The true Christian life which was displayed shook the entire city of Jerusalem and soon spread to other cities and villages. Then, as Jesus predicted, the false seeds of Satan's weeds took root and began to appear, not only as counterfeit Christians within the church, but as sin and counterfeit Christianity in the lives of true Christians (see the story of Ananias and Sapphira in Acts 5; the story of Simon Magus in Acts 8).

Once these weeds began to appear, it became the task of the apostles to instruct Christians about how to recognize the counterfeit Christianity that was in them along with the true, so that they could purify themselves, repudiating sin by the power of the crucified Lord while yielding themselves by faith to the resurrection life and power of Jesus Christ. Inspired by the Holy Spirit, the early apostles developed and laid down the pattern of operation intended by the Lord for His body, the church. This timeless pattern, when closely followed, would make the church of any age, of any millennium, the most powerful force on earth!

Invisible and visible governments

Do we truly realize the power that is available to us? Do we have any concept of the power Jesus intended for His church to wield in this dark and dangerous world? Or has our vision of the church become so dimmed that the word *church* suggests to us only a building on the corner where we go once a week to sing hymns and hear sermons?

The church, as God designed it and as the Bible describes it, is an amazing, dynamic, world-changing force. It is, in fact, a kind of invisible government, influencing and moving the visible governments of the earth. Because of the powerful influence of the church, the people of this planet are able to experience the benefits of social stability, law and order, justice and peace. Yes, the world is troubled and in turmoil—but we haven't seen even a fraction of one percent of the tribulation, tyranny, anarchy, and slaughter that would take place if the church were suddenly taken out of this world! (See Matthew 5:13–14; Philippians 2:14–15; 1 Timothy 2:1–2.)

Whenever the church has followed the biblical pattern and become more of what God designed it to be, righteous conditions have spread throughout society. When the church has abandoned this divine pattern, relying on worldly power, becoming proud, rich, and tyrannical, then it has become weak and despised—and the terrible forces of evil have been unleashed in the world.

"When all else fails, follow directions!" says the popular slogan. God has given us a set of directions for building a powerful, functional, dynamically effective church. In this book, we will open the

Scriptures and examine God's directions for the church—which, as it turns out, are also God's directions for building a rewarding, effective, dynamic life. It is through the *koinonia*-fellowship of the church that we truly become all God intended us to be.

We find God's truth and instructions about His church throughout the New Testament, and especially in the writings of the apostle Paul—his letters are, after all, written specifically to individual churches and to church leaders, such as Timothy and Titus. Paul's masterpiece of the church is his letter to the Ephesians, which deals almost exclusively with the origin, nature, and function of the church, and its essential relationship to the Lord. So it is to this letter that we now turn, and especially to the first sixteen verses of chapter 4. There we will find our guideline to God's truth about the life of the body of Christ, the church.

CHAPTER 2

THE CHURCH'S HIGHEST PRIORITY

This is a revolutionary age.

The hurricane winds of change are howling around the world. The human race seethes with unrest and rebellion. Our political institutions are polarized, divided to the left and right with little common ground in the center. Despite the signs of current prosperity, our debt-ridden, hair-triggered economy seems destined to collapse. We have barred and deadbolted our homes, making ourselves prisoners, while in our neighborhoods criminals roam free, grafitti-tagging and shooting at random, filling our hearts with fear. With every day's headlines, with every new atrocity or terrorist attack, we see more evidence that there is a very thin line that separates civilization from anarchy. We seem to be approaching not just a political breakdown, but a cultural meltdown.

What is our response? Is there anything the church can do in the face of such complex and insoluble problems? Can the church make a difference in this wobbly, dangerous world? Or has the church simply become irrelevant?

Amazingly, when Paul wrote his letter to the Christians at the city of Ephesus, the Christians of the first century faced strikingly similar problems and asked similar questions. Ephesus was a city in the Roman province of Asia, and the entire Roman Empire was being shaken by political instability, civil unrest, crime, and radical change. Half the population of the empire were slaves, sunk into such hopeless bondage that they were traded and sold like cattle. Except for a small class of rich aristocrats and patricians, most of the population eked out a poverty-line living as farmers, tradespeople, and laborers.

The moral corruption of Ephesus was legendary. The city was the center of worship for the sex-goddess, Diana of the Ephesians. As for cruelty, the Roman legions were ready to march anywhere to suppress any rebellion or civil disorder with ruthless slaughter. The ruler of the Roman world was Emperor Nero, whose sordid and savage life had scandalized the empire.

Paul was in Rome, a prisoner of Caesar, when he wrote his letter to the Ephesians. He was awaiting the hour when he would be summoned before Nero. Though permitted to live in his own rented house, Paul could not go about the city. Instead, he was subjected to the indignity of being chained day and night to a Roman guard. Seeing about him the decadent life of the city, and knowing the conditions that prevailed in distant Ephesus, what would the apostle tell the Christians to do when he wrote? The answer is striking and instructive: "I therefore, a prisoner for the Lord, beg you to lead a life worthy of the calling to which you have been called, with all lowliness and meekness, with patience, forbearing one another in love, eager to maintain the unity of the Spirit in the bond of peace" (Ephesians 4:1–3).

What does the apostle say to the Ephesian church in the face of so many desperate cries of human need? What is his answer to the pleas for justice and relief from oppression all around him? Simply this: *Fulfill your calling! Obey your orders! Don't deviate from the divine strategy! Follow your Lord!*

In this admonition the apostle clearly recognizes the true nature and function of the church. It is not a human institution. It is not expected to devise its own strategy and set its own goals. It is not an independent organization, existing by means of the strength of its numbers. It is, rather, a body called into a special relationship to God. Within this letter to the Ephesians, the apostle employs several word-pictures to describe the relationship between God and the church:

• **A body:** Paul says the church is a body under the control of its Head. What a tragedy it would be if that body refused to respond to the direction of its Head! In the realm of medicine, there are diseases which ravage the nerve pathways that enable the human brain to control the human body. It is tragic and heartbreaking to see a person bound to a wheelchair or hospital bed, unable to control his movements and body functions. A church that is unresponsive to its Head is every bit as tragic and heartbreaking to watch.

• **A temple:** The church is also a temple for the exclusive habitation and use of a Person who dwells within, and who has the right to do with that temple whatever He wills.

• **An army:** The church is an army under the command of a king. An army that will not obey its leader is useless as a fighting force. Therefore, says Paul to the church, obey your orders, follow your Leader.

The divine strategy

Paul didn't just preach to the Ephesians. He was an example to them. After languishing for two years as a prisoner in Caesarea, Palestine, he had been sent to Rome on a perilous sea voyage that ended in shipwreck on the island of Malta. Finally, he arrived at Rome, a prisoner of the Roman emperor. Yet never once in his letter does he refer to himself as "the prisoner of Caesar." He always calls himself "a prisoner of [or for] the Lord." He does not fret about being chained up in prison. Read his letter to the Philippians (which was also written from prison in Rome), and you'll find it glows with an aura of joy and the assurance of ultimate triumph.

Paul does not consider himself a prisoner of Caesar. The Roman emperor may think he runs the world and everyone in it, but there is a much higher Authority in charge. Behind Caesar is Christ, and Caesar can do nothing to Paul unless the Lord Jesus Christ allows it. Paul sees beyond the chains and the guard and the imperial processes of justice—and what he sees there is the controlling hand of Jesus Christ.

In his letter to the Corinthians, Paul says, "We look not to the things that are seen but to the things that are unseen" (2 Corinthians 4:18). Why? Because that is where the ultimate answers lie. That is where ultimate truth is found, where the ultimate power exists. Jesus Himself reflected this same attitude when He stood before Pontius Pilate.

Pilate said to Him, "Do you not know that I have power . . . to crucify you?" Jesus replied immediately, "You would have no power over me unless it had been given you from above" (John 19:10–11).

Much of the explanation for the confusion that exists so widely in the church today is that Christians have been looking at the things seen instead of at the things that are unseen. We see a suffering world with human need groaning and screaming everywhere. Hate and bigotry abound, injustice prevails and misery exists wherever we turn. The obvious solution: Let's get to work—now! What are we waiting for? Let's do something—*anything!*

It sounds so logical—but that is because our human thinking is shallow and superficial. We see only the things that are visible. In our shallow concern for externals we treat symptoms and not causes. We apply superficial remedies that work only for the moment, if they work at all. Soon the situation is worse than before—and we wonder why.

We desperately need this practical admonition of the apostle: "Lead a life worthy of the calling to which you have been called" (Ephesians 4:1). The One who has called us sees life much more clearly than we do. He has devised a strategy that will actually remove the root cause of human darkness and misery—not just cover the cancer of sin with a Band-Aid. When the church is faithful to its calling, it becomes a healing agency in society, able to lift a whole nation or an empire to a higher plateau of healthy, wholesome living.

In his monumental history of the world, *The Story of Civilization,* Will Durant compares the influence of Caesar and Christ. He says of Jesus:

> The revolution He sought was a far deeper one, without which reforms could be only superficial and transitory. If He could cleanse the human heart of selfish desire, cruelty, and lust, utopia would come of itself, and all those institutions that rise out of human greed and violence, and the consequent need for law, would disappear. Since this would be the profoundest of all revolutions, beside which all others would be mere coup d'etats of class ousting class and exploiting in its turn, Christ was, in this spiritual sense the greatest revolutionist in history.[1]

The true church is here to effect that revolution. The false church is here to oppose it. But true Christians actually promote the cause of false Christianity when, through ignorance or mistaken zeal, they deviate from the divine strategy and disobey their divine calling. We mere humans cannot improve on the divine program. Nor are we left in doubt as to what that calling is. The first three chapters of Ephesians are devoted to describing it, and it is also detailed elsewhere throughout the New Testament. If Christians are to give intelligent obedience to their Lord, they must give highest priority to understanding what He wants them to be and do.

Back to reality

Human strategies are founded upon limited human understanding and the best estimates human beings can make. But God's strategy, His calling upon our lives, is based upon an absolutely perfect understanding of fundamental and ultimate reality. In fact, that is the glory of Christianity: it sets forth things as they really are. The Christian diagnosis of all the world's ills—from conflicts between nations to conflicts within an individual human soul—is accurate because it reflects a true understanding of the human condition.

The New Testament epistles always begin with the truth—what we call "doctrine." The New Testament writers always call us back to reality. Then, on the basis of that underlying foundation of truth, they go on to suggest certain practical applications. How foolish it is to start with anything but truth!

In the opening chapters of Ephesians, Paul makes several clear statements regarding the purpose of the church—and not merely its purpose for eternity, off in misty futurity, but its purpose right *here*, right *now*. Let's examine some of these statements of the nature and purpose of the church.

Purpose No. 1: *The church is to reflect God's holiness.*

"He chose us in him [Christ] before the foundation of the world, that we should be holy and blameless before him" (Ephesians 1:4). Here we see clearly that the church is no afterthought with God. It was planned long before the world was made.

And what is God's first concern for the church? He is not, first of all, concerned with what the church *does*, but with what the church *is*. *Being* must always precede *doing*, for what we *are* determines what we *do*. To understand the moral character of God's people is essential to understanding the nature of the church. As Christians, we are to be a moral example to the world, reflecting the pure character and holiness of Jesus Christ.

A number of years ago, a father received a letter from his son, who was away at a Christian college. "Dear Dad," the letter began. "I'm sending you this letter absolutely free! The post office didn't cancel the stamp on your last letter to me, so I peeled it off and used it again!"

A short time later, the son received a letter from his father. The young man ripped open the envelope. Imagine his surprise when he saw that his father had pasted a brand-new postage stamp at the top of the letter—then he had inked a big, bold **X** over it so the stamp couldn't be used again. Beneath the stamp, in his father's handwriting, were these words:

"Dear Son, your debt to the United States government has been paid."

This Christian father set an example for his son that the young man never forgot: Our goal as Christians is to be people of unbending, uncompromising character and integrity. If we refuse to compromise our integrity and morality in the smallest details, then we will be faithful in the bigger things.

As Howard Hendricks puts it, "You show me a leader who is great in public and I will show you a leader who is even greater in private." As Christians, we are called to be "holy and blameless" before God, both inside and out. We are to reflect His holiness. That is one of the purposes of the church. When our inner self is seamlessly bonded to our outer self, then we will project the purity and right-eousness of God to a watching world.

Purpose No. 2: *The church is to reveal God's glory.*

Paul gives us another purpose of the church in the first chapter of Ephesians:

"He destined us in love to be his sons through Jesus Christ, according to the purpose of his will, to the praise of his glorious grace" (verse 5).

"We who first hoped in Christ have been destined and appointed to live for the praise of his glory" (verse 12).

Think of that! The phrase "we who first hoped in Christ" refers to us who are Christians as having been destined and appointed to live for the praise of His glory. The first task of the church is not the welfare of human beings. Yes, our welfare is definitely important to God, but that is not the church's first task. Rather, we have been chosen by God to live to the praise and glory of God, so that through our lives His glory will be revealed to the world. As the New English Bible states it, "We should cause his glory to be praised."

What is God's glory? It is God Himself, the revelation of what God is and does. The problem with this world is that it does not know God. It has no understanding of Him. In all its seekings and wanderings, its endeavors to discover truth, it does not know God. But the glory of God is to reveal Himself, to show the world what He Himself is like. And when the works of God and the nature of God are demonstrated through the church, He is glorified. As Paul writes in 2 Corinthians, "For it is the God who said, 'Let light shine out of darkness,' who has shone in our hearts to give the light of the knowledge of the glory of God in the face of Christ" (2 Corinthians 4:6).

People can see the glory of God in the face of Christ, in His character, His being. And that glory is also found, says Paul, in "our hearts." God calls the church to reveal to the world the glory of His character, which is found in the face of Jesus Christ. This is stated again in chapter 1 of Ephesians: "He has put all things under his [Christ's] feet and has made him the head over all things for the church, which is his body, the fullness of him who fills all in all" (Ephesians 1:22–23).

That is a tremendous statement! Here, Paul says that all that Jesus Christ is (His fullness) is to be seen in His body, which is the church! The secret of the church is that Christ lives in it and the message of the church to the world is to declare Him, to talk about Jesus Christ. Paul describes this secret of the true church again in the second chapter of Ephesians: "So then you are no longer strangers and sojourners, but you are fellow citizens with the saints and members of the household of God, built upon the foundation of the apostles and prophets, Christ Jesus himself being the chief cornerstone, in whom the whole structure is joined together and grows into a holy temple in the Lord; in whom you also are built into it for a dwelling place of God in the Spirit" (Ephesians 2:19–22).

There is the holy mystery of the church—it is the dwelling place of God. He lives in His people. That is the great calling of the church—to make visible the invisible Christ. Paul describes his own ministry as a model Christian in these terms: "To make all men see what is the plan of the mystery hidden for ages in God who created all things; that through the church the manifold wisdom of God might now be made known to the principalities and powers in the heavenly places" (Ephesians 3:9–10).

There it is. The task of the church is "to make

known the manifold wisdom of God," to make it known not only to human beings but also to angels who are observing the church. These are "the principalities and powers in the heavenly places." There are others besides human beings watching the church and learning from it.

Surely the verses above are enough to make one thing perfectly clear. The calling of the church is to declare in word and demonstrate in deed the character of Christ who lives within His people. We are to declare the reality of a life-changing encounter with a living Christ and to demonstrate that change by an unselfish, love-filled life. Until we have done that, nothing else we can do will be effective for God. That is the calling of the church Paul talks about when he writes, "I beg you to lead a life worthy of the calling to which you have been called" (Ephesians 4:1).

Notice how the Lord Jesus Himself confirms this calling in the opening chapter of the book of Acts. Just before Jesus ascended to His Father, He said to His disciples: "You shall receive power when the Holy Spirit has come upon you; and you shall be my witnesses in Jerusalem and in all Judea and Samaria and to the end of the earth" (Acts 1:8).

Purpose No. 3: *The church is to be a witness to Christ.*

The church is called to be a witness, and a witness is one who declares and demonstrates. The apostle Peter has a wonderful word about the church's witnessing role in his first letter: "You are a chosen race, a royal priesthood, a holy nation, God's own people, that you may declare the wonderful deeds of him who called you out of darkness into his marvelous light" (1 Peter 2:9).

Notice the structure, "You are . . . that you may." That is our primary task as Christians. We are indwelt by Jesus Christ so that we may demonstrate the life and character of the One who lives within. The responsibility to fulfill this calling of the church belongs to every true Christian. All are called, all are indwelt by the Holy Spirit, all are expected to fulfill their calling in the midst of the world. That is the clear note the apostle sounds throughout the whole Ephesian letter. The expression of the church's witness may sometimes be corporate, but the responsibility to witness is always individual. It is your responsibility and mine.

But here a problem re-emerges: the problem of possible counterfeit Christians. It is easy for the church (or the individual Christian) to talk about displaying the character of Christ and to make grandiose claims about doing so. However, as many knowledgeable pagans know from observing Christians closely, the image Christians project is not always the true, biblical image of Jesus Christ. That is why the apostle Paul is careful to describe authentic Christlike character in more specific terms: "With all lowliness and meekness, with patience, forbearing one another in love, eager to maintain the unity of the Spirit in the bond of peace" (Ephesians 4:2–3).

Humility, patience, love, unity, and peace—these are the true marks of Jesus. Christians are to witness, but not arrogantly or rudely, not with an attitude of holier-than-thou smugness, not in sanctimonious presumption, and certainly not against a background of ugly church fights, Christian against Christian. The church is not to talk about itself. It is to be lowly in mind, not boasting of its power or seeking to advance its prestige. The church cannot save the world—but the Lord of the church can. It is not the church for which Christians are to labor and spend their lives, but for the Lord of the church.

The church cannot exalt its Lord while it seeks to exalt itself. The true church does not seek to gain power in the eyes of the world. It already has all the power it needs from the Lord who indwells it.

Further, the church is to be patient and forbearing, knowing that the seeds of truth take time to sprout, time to grow, and time to come to full harvest. The church is not to *demand* that society make sudden, tearing changes in long-established social patterns. Rather, the church is to exemplify positive social change by shunning evil and practicing righteousness, and thus planting seeds of truth which will take root in society and ultimately produce the fruit of change.

The supreme mark
of the authentic Christian

In *The Decline and Fall of the Roman Empire,* historian Edward Gibbon ascribes the collapse of Rome not to invading enemies, but to disintegration from within. In that book is a passage Sir Winston Churchill committed to memory because he felt it was so instructive and accurate. It is significant that this passage talks about the role of the church within the declining empire:

> While that great body [the Roman Empire] was invaded by open violence or undermined by slow decay, a pure and humble religion gently insinuated itself into the minds of men, grew up in silence and obscurity, derived new vigor from opposition, and finally erected the triumphant banner of the Cross on the ruins of the Capitol.[2]

How was the Christian faith able to conquer the Roman Empire? Did the early Christians undermine and subvert the Roman government with plots and hidden agendas? Unthinkable! Did the Christians brainwash the minds of the Roman people with clever propaganda? Of course not! Well, did the Christians come against the Romans with superior weapons and larger armies, subduing the Roman Empire by force? Ridiculous!

The early Christians had only *one* strategy, *one* agenda, *one* message, *one* weapon, *one* force with which to overwhelm the empire of the caesars: *love.* It was Christlike love that brought the empire to its knees, and erected the symbol of the cross over the ruins of the Roman Capitol. Love was an unstoppable force in the first century A.D., and it is just a irresistible today.

The supreme mark of the life of Jesus Christ within the Christian is, of course, *love.* Love that accepts others as they are. Love that is tenderhearted and forgiving. Love that seeks to heal misunderstandings, divisions, and broken relationships. Jesus said, "By this all men will know that you are my disciples, if you have love for one another" (John 13:35). That love is never manifested by rivalry, greed, flashy display, indifference, or prejudice. It is the very opposite of name-calling, backbiting, stubbornness, and division.

Here we discover the unifying force that enables the church to carry out its purpose in the world: *Christlike love.* How do we reflect God's holiness? *By our love!* How do we reveal God's glory? By our love! How do we witness to the reality of Jesus Christ? *By our love!*

The New Testament has very little to say about Christian involvement in politics or defending "family values" or promoting peace and justice or opposing pornography or defending the rights of this or that oppressed group. I'm not saying Christians should not be concerned about these issues. Obviously you cannot have a heart filled with love for human beings and not be concerned about these things. But the New Testament says relatively little about these things because God knows that the only way to solve these problems and heal broken relationships is by introducing a *totally new dynamic* into human life—the dynamic of the life of Jesus Christ.

The life of Jesus Christ is what men and women truly need. The elimination of darkness begins with the introduction of light. The elimination of hatred begins with the introduction of love. The elimination of sickness and corruption begins with the introduction of life. We must begin with the introduction of Christ, for that is the cause to which we are called.

The gospel germinated in a social climate much like our own—a time of injustice, racial division, social unrest, rampant crime, unbridled immorality, economic uncertainty, and widespread fear. The early Christian church struggled to survive under persecution so relentless and murderous it is beyond our ability to imagine. But the early church did not see its calling as one of fighting injustice and oppression, or demanding its "rights." The early church saw its mission as one of reflecting God's holiness, revealing God's glory, and witnessing to the reality of Jesus Christ—and it did so by demonstrating *relentless love*, both toward those within the fellowship, and those outside.

The outside of the cup

Those who look for proof texts to justify picketing, protests, boycotts, and other "in-your-face" political action to cure social ills are doomed to disappointment. Jesus called this "washing the outside of the cup." A true Christian revolution changes people from the inside. It cleanses the inside of the cup.

This is where churches so often go astray. They become obsessed with a political agenda. Christ came to transform society—but He didn't come to do so through political action. His plan was to *change society by transforming the individual people in that society*—by giving them a new heart, a new spirit, a new orientation, a new direction, a new birth, a resurrection life, and the death of self and selfishness. Once you transform the individuals, you will have a new society.

When we are changed from within, when the inside of the cup is cleansed, our entire outlook on human relationships changes. Our natural inclination, when confronted with conflict and mistreatment, is to respond with "an eye for an eye." But Jesus calls us to a new kind of response: "Bless those who persecute you." This is the response the apostle Paul calls us to when he writes, "Live in harmony with one another. . . . Repay no one evil for evil. . . . Do not be overcome by evil, but overcome evil with good" (Romans 12:14–21).

The message God has entrusted to the church is the most revolutionary message the world has ever heard. Should we now surrender that message in favor of mere political and social action? Should we content ourselves with allowing the church to become just another worldly political or social organization? Do we believe God enough to agree with Him that it is Christlike love, lived out in the *koinonia*-community of His church, that will change the world—not political power or social agendas?

God calls us to become individually responsible to spread the radical, revolutionary, life-transforming good news of Jesus Christ throughout society. The church must again invade commercial and industrial life, education and learning, the arts and family life, government and social institutions with this tremendous, transforming, unequaled message.

The risen Lord Jesus Christ has come among us to implant His own never-ending life within us. He is ready and able to transform us into loving, compassionate, confident people, empowered to cope with any problem, any challenge life sets before us. That is our message to a weary, fearful, sorrowing world. That is the message of love and hope we bring to a hostile and despairing world.

We exist to reflect God's holiness, to reveal God's glory, and to witness to the fact that Jesus has come to cleanse men and women, inside and out. We exist to love one another, and to demonstrate Christlike love to the world. That is our purpose. That is the calling of the church.

CHAPTER 3

NOT UNION— UNITY!

In one of her *Anne of Green Gables* novels, Lucy Maud Montgomery relates a story of a cranky old churchwoman named Aunt Atossa. At Sunday evening prayer services in Aunt Atossa's church, the members would stand and pray in turn or share a prayer need or praise report. It happened that one of these services was led by a visiting minister—a very kind and spiritual man, but also very deaf! He would lean toward each person who stood and spoke, and he would appear to be very attentive, but he could scarcely understand a word that was said!

At this service, cantankerous old Aunt Atossa—who had been storing up a trunkful of grievances and bitterness in her heart for years—finally decided to unload. After a few people stood to pray or share prayer requests, Aunt Atossa jumped to her feet and loudly raked the congregation up one side and down the other. She called out various parishioners by name and accused them of various sins. She castigated every church member with whom she had ever had a quarrel or disagreement (which was practically everyone). She ripped the lids off of several church scandals, causing several of the ladies in the surrounding pews to collapse in a swoon.

"I'm so disgusted with this church," she concluded fiercely, "that after I leave tonight, I intend to never darken its door again! May God bring a fearful judgment on all of you!" Then, finally out of breath and out of hateful words to say, she sat down.

At the pulpit, the kindly, hard-of-hearing minister smiled benignly, nodded gently, and said in a very pious voice, "Amen! The Lord grant our dear sister's prayer!"[1]

There's no question that one of the most destructive forces in the church today is conflict between Christians. Division among brothers and sisters has destroyed churches, destroyed lives, and brought the gospel of Jesus Christ into disrepute. So it is not surprising that we hear many voices today saying, "If the church is to fulfill its calling, Christians must live in union together. We can't change the world as long as we are fragmented and divided. In our disunity, we really have nothing to say to the world. Our disunity makes us weak, and it causes us to be a laughingstock in our society. There is power in numbers, and if we can unite all of our different factions into a single Christian force, we can influence society as we were intended to do."

This philosophy gave rise to the ecumenical movement of the latter part of the twentieth century. The word *ecumenical* comes from the Greek word *oikumene*, which originally meant "the entire inhabited world," and it has come to mean "universal, of worldwide scope." The hope and dream of those in the modern ecumenical movement is to dissolve the differences among Christians, as represented by the variety of denominations we have today, and to bring about a truly ecumenical—that is, universal—church.

The words of the apostle Paul in Ephesians do stress the need for Christian unity. He exhorts the Ephesian Christians to be "eager to maintain the unity of the Spirit in the bond of peace" (Ephesians 4:3). This is one of a number of Scripture passages which underscore the need for Christian agreement. The ecumenicists say that when the churches unite in one organization it will be the fulfillment of the prayer of Jesus: "That they all may be one, as thou, Father, art in me, and I in thee, that they also may be one in us: that the world may believe that thou hast sent me" (John 17:21 KJV). "Why not welcome these modern efforts to produce that unity?" ask the one-world church advocates. "Surely the union of all Christians can only strengthen and help the cause of Christ!"

A glorious mixture

What shall we make of Paul's exhortation of to unity? One thing is clear: Paul explicitly recognizes the reality of friction among Christians. He would not urge Christians to "maintain the unity of the Spirit" if there were not differences existing among them. There were obviously forces at work in the early church to divide the Christian body. There were pressures among them to break up into splinter groups.

To counteract these pressures, the apostle urged them to be "eager to maintain the unity." The word *eager* is a bit too weak here. Eagerness implies mere willingness, but the original Greek word suggests willingness plus action. Paul is saying, "Be proactive! Take positive, aggressive action to maintain unity!" The King James translation is more accurate in this regard: "endeavoring to keep the unity of the Spirit in the bond of peace."

Certainly it is unrealistic for Christians to pretend there are no differences among them. There is no group in the world so gloriously diverse and heterogeneous as the church. The genius of the church is that it is made up of so many different kinds of people. In the true church of Christ, the rich and poor gather on the same footing, without distinction, without favoritism; in Christ, there is no distinction between Jews or Gentiles, men or women, black, white, or any other color (see 1 Corinthians 12:13; Galatians 3:28; Colossians 3:11; James 2:1–6).

This, admittedly, is not the way the church has always behaved, but this *is* the way the church was *meant* to be and *can* be. The church crosses all the boundaries men erect. It transcends all natural distinctions as well, gathering all people into a single body, without any exceptions or exclusions. Few other assemblies in the world attempt to unite people from such widely varied origins and backgrounds.

But we do not ignore these boundaries easily. Friction arises over our differences in the body of Christ. It is clear from the Scriptures that friction has existed in the Christian community since the first century. There was the great disagreement over the relationship between Gentile believers and Jewish believers in the early church—a disagreement which directly led to the great Council of Jerusalem described in Acts 15. In Paul's letter to the Philippians two women are mentioned who had difficulty getting along with each other. Their names were Euodia and Syntyche (or, as they have sometimes been rendered, Odious and Soon-Touchy). Disagreements and personality differences continue to be a source of friction in the church today—hence the anonymous lines:

> To dwell above with saints we love,
> Oh that will be glory.
> But to live below, with saints we know—
> Well, that's another story!

Besides differences of viewpoints and personalities, there are differences of gifts within the body of Christ. Let's be honest: We Christians have an unfortunate tendency to disparage the gifts of other believers and to exalt our own. We all feel that what we are contributing is more important and more valuable than what others are doing—and this, too, is no new wrinkle in the church. In 1 Corinthians 3, we see a division in the church of Corinth brought about as the followers of one teacher-leader take sides against the followers of another. Clearly, the church is fertile ground for friction over differences, distinctions, and diversity.

But also embedded in Paul's message to the Ephesian church is a powerful implication: Despite the differences between the early Christians, there is also a basic, underlying unity. It is not a unity that the believers themselves have produced. In fact, nowhere does the apostle tell the believers that they should strive to produce unity. Instead—and this is crucially important to understand—he tells them to *maintain the unity that is already there!*

The church is *never* told to create unity. There is a unity that exists in the church by virtue of the simple fact that the church exists. We human beings are incapable of producing this unity which is so essential to the life of the body. Where does this unity come from? It can only be produced by the Spirit of God. But once produced, Christians are responsible to *maintain* it. And maintain this unity through Christlike love.

Sevenfold unity

That's the problem with the modern ecumenical movement: It doesn't understand where unity comes from, or that the unity Paul talks about already exists! Instead, the ecumenicists try to manufacture a semblance of unity—not the true *unity* of the Spirit, but an external, organizational *union* of Christians. Unity is a spiritual, godly quality. Union is an institutional, worldly entity. Unity is something God produces and we maintain. Union is something human beings construct out of their own efforts.

The tragedy of ecumenical unionism is that it ignores and attempts to supplant the true unity that God has already given to the church. That is why Paul takes such pains to make sure no one misunderstands the true nature of the unity of the Spirit, writing, "There is one body, and one Spirit, just as you were called to the one hope that belongs to your call, one Lord, one faith, one baptism, one God and Father of us all, who is above all and through all and in all" (Ephesians 4:4–6).

Here is the true unity of the body of Christ. Notice, first of all, that Paul here expresses a sevenfold unity: one body, one Spirit, one hope, one Lord, one faith, one baptism, one God and Father of us all. Notice, next, that this sevenfold unity gathers around the three Persons of the Trinity: Spirit, Son, and Father. It is a body indwelt by the Triune God. Here we clearly see the Father's answer to His Son's prayer in Gethsemane: "That they may all be one; even as thou, Father, art in me, and I in thee" (John 17:21).

The church is not to be a conglomeration of individuals who happen to agree upon certain ideas. It is bound together as an organism in a bodily unity. It is true that a body is an organization, but it is much more than an organization. The essence of a body is that it consists of thousands of cells with one mutually shared life.

We've all heard the words of the old spiritual:

> *The toe bone's connected to the foot bone,*
> *The foot bone's connected to the ankle bone,*
> *The ankle bone's connected to the shin bone,*
> *Now hear the Word of the Lord!*

It's a catchy song, but the theology is not quite correct. You don't produce a body by combining bits and pieces of anatomy together. A body is formed by the growth and multiplication of many cells from one original cell. The body grows cell by cell until a mature body grows—but every one of those cells shares the life of that one original cell, and the life of every other cell in the body. That is the secret of the body: all parts of the body share life together.

It is the sharing of life that makes a body different from an organization. An organization derives power from the association of individuals, but a body derives its power from the sharing of life. As Dr. Bernard Ramm observes:

> When modernists deny . . . a supernatural connectedness
> of all believers by the mystical union of the Holy Spirit,
> they destroy the historic, orthodox Christian
> understanding of the Church. . . . [Thus] the Church
> becomes a society, a natural, human, non-supernatural
> religious community. It is bound together by purely
> natural ties, such as a common heritage in the Bible, a
> common belief in some sort of uniqueness in Jesus, a
> common belief in the historical continuity of Christians,
> and a common ethic of love. Now the church is a society.
> But this is secondary to its being the supernatural body of
> Christ.[2]

Anyone who has had the privilege of contacting
Christians in widespread places around the earth soon
learns to recognize the fundamental unity of the Spirit
which already exists among all true Christians.
Whatever the denominational, theological, political,
geographical, or cultural differences between
ourselves and another believer, the mutual life in
Christ is immediately evident. There is a sense of
belonging to each other. This unity is often discernible
even when there is an official denial of it.

I once met with a Roman Catholic bishop in
Mexico and spent an hour or two with him, talking
about Christ. I was a Protestant and he a Catholic, and
if we had gone into doctrinal areas we would have
found many differences of outlook. But with this
particular bishop I immediately sensed a oneness
which we shared together in Christ. He knew the
reality of the living Lord, just as I did. So while our
organizations and affiliations were not the same, we
were one together because we had entered into that
beautiful experience of the unity of the Spirit.

The power of the church

This brings us to the next element in Paul's description of the unity of the church: one Spirit. This is the great, eternal, invisible Person who is the true power of the church. The strength of the church never derives from its numbers. The ecumenicists seek to create a unity of the flesh, an organizational unity that draws its power from many bodies joined together, quite apart from conviction and spiritual agreement. But the power of the church to influence society does not derive from gathering together enough Christians to swing enough votes to sway a legislature. God's plan will not be achieved by worldly power.

The prophet Zechariah was once confronted with a great mountain which God said would become a plain. When Zechariah began to look around to see how this would happen and where the power would come from to level that mountain to a plain, the word of the Lord came to him: "Not by might, nor by power, but by my Spirit, says the LORD of hosts" (Zechariah 4:6).

Impossible tasks require superhuman power. Since the role of the church in the world is far beyond the powers of mere men and women to fulfill, it is essential that the church rely on the only adequate power available. The Spirit is the true power of the church. There is only one Spirit. He is the same everywhere, no matter where the church exists, in every place and in every age. The Spirit does not change, and that is why truth remains unchangeable. The passing of time does not affect it.

This is also why the church is not dependent on many or on few, or on the wisdom of its membership.

The church is to trust and depend on one thing only: the Spirit of God. As we move deeper into the apostle's message to the Ephesian church, we shall learn more about how this amazing power works.

"There is one body and one Spirit," says Paul in Ephesians 4:4—and then he goes on to link the Spirit to the hope we have in Christ: "just as you were called to the one hope that belongs to your call." Do you see how these three factors of unity are all linked together? *One* body. *One* Spirit. *One* hope. What is that hope? It is expressed dozens of times throughout the Scriptures: the hope of the return of Jesus Christ to earth! The Spirit forms the body in order that the body may achieve its final and ultimate goal—its redemption, and the sharing of Christ's glory when He returns.

Perhaps the most succinct expression of this hope is found in Colossians, where Paul writes, "Christ in you, the hope of glory" (1:27). Glory is the hope of the church. As John puts it, "We know that when he appears we shall be like him, for we shall see him as he is. And every one who thus hopes in him purifies himself as he is pure" (1 John 3:2–3).

Everywhere I've traveled around the world, I've found this to be the hope of Christians. No matter what their denomination, their background, their race, or their color this is always the one hope: that they will someday be like Christ. There are many differences in understanding how this will work out. Some are premillenialists (believing that Christ will come before the millennium, the thousand-year reign of Christ on earth). Others are post-millennialists (believing that Christ will return after the millennium). Still others do not believe in a millennium at all. But there is only one final expectation of Christians everywhere—that they will share the glory of Christ.

No other name

The apostle Paul next gathers up three more elements of unity around the second Person of the Trinity, the *one Lord*. He does not say "one Savior," though it is true there is only one Savior. Everywhere in Scripture, it is only when people acknowledge Jesus as Lord that He becomes their Savior. The fundamental issue Paul centers on is that Jesus Christ is Lord. In writing to the Corinthians he says that no one can say "Jesus is Lord" except by the Holy Spirit.

Lord means ultimate authority. To call Jesus *Lord* is to recognize that He is the supreme person in the universe. There is no other Lord, and there never will be another Lord. Peter puts it bluntly in Acts 4:12: "There is no other name under heaven, given among men by which we must be saved." That is why the early Christians could not say "Caesar is Lord" as their Roman persecutors tried to force them to say. That is why modern Christians cannot say, "Buddha is Lord," or that any other person is Lord but Jesus.

The mystery and marvel of this man Christ Jesus—who lived and walked and loved and worked and died among men, whose life record is given to us in the Gospels—is also Lord of the Universe, the Supreme Being, Creator of all things, the God-man. The apostle John, in his first letter, says that anyone who denies this is not a Christian, but has the spirit of antichrist (1 John 2:22).

And Paul declares, "Therefore God has highly exalted him and bestowed on him the name which is above every name, that at the name of Jesus every knee should bow, in heaven and on earth and under the earth, and every tongue confess that Jesus Christ is Lord, to the glory of God the Father" (Philippians 2:9–11).

One faith

Linked to this is the next element, *one faith*. This is a little more difficult to understand, but it seems clear that Paul does not refer to faith in general. That is, Paul is not talking here about the ability to believe, because all human beings have this. Sometimes people say, "I can't believe." But this is clearly untrue, because people are believing all the time. All action comes from belief. An atheist acts from belief, just as a Christian does. They both believe something and act accordingly.

Nor does Paul, in talking of *one faith*, mean the act of conversion when a person declares himself out and out for Christ—the initial step of believing and trusting in Him which we call "saving faith." Paul is not speaking of these kinds of faith here. He has in view that which is believed—that is, the body of truth which has been revealed. There is but one faith. This one faith is what Jude refers to in his letter when he exhorts Christians, "Contend for the faith which was once for all delivered to the saints" (Jude 1:3).

This one faith is associated with Jesus the Lord. It is the truth about Him. Again, there may be differences of opinion among Christians of goodwill as to doctrinal details and biblical interpretations, but everywhere there is full agreement among true Christians that there is but one body of truth about Jesus Christ. There is only one set of facts, one faith. That body of truth is the Scripture.

There is not a faith for Jews and another set of facts for Gentiles; there is only one faith for all people everywhere. God has spoken through the seers, the prophets and the apostles, but it all forms one total picture, articulated and explaining itself. There is not, therefore, a God of the Old Testament versus a God of the New Testament, as we sometimes hear. Nor can we say, as some people say, "Well, I have my Christ, and you have yours." No, there is only one Christ. There is but one historic Jesus. There is but one faith.

One baptism

The next element of unity is the *one baptism.*

You may well wonder, "Unity—about *baptism?!*" Nothing could seem farther from reality. All varieties of Baptists say, "This 'one baptism' surely refers to water baptism, which is by immersion only." The Presbyterians say, "No, the Baptists are all wet! Sprinkling is the only proper way." Some groups insist that baptism is for infants only while others say that it must be performed only upon adults who understand the meaning of faith and baptism. There seems to be anything but unity on the question of baptism!

But despite these obvious differences over the symbol of baptism, there is *one baptism* everywhere recognized and agreed upon by the church: the baptism of the Spirit, the real baptism, of which water baptism is the symbol. It is the means by which every true believer in Jesus Christ is made part of His living body, the church (see 1 Corinthians 12:13). That baptism is here linked to Jesus Christ, the Lord, because it is baptism into His body. Romans 6:3 puts it this way: We were all "baptized into his death." The central idea is that each individual believer is made to be one with Jesus Christ, united with Him in His death and His resurrection.

Our Father

In Ephesians 4:6, the apostle gives us the last of the seven elements of unity: "One God and Father of us all, who is above all and through all and in all." Here is the ultimate aim of all the other unities. All of the rest exist, as Peter puts it, to "bring us to God" (1 Peter 3:18). He is the goal and the aim.

The sign that we have truly found God is that we recognize Him as Father, we sense His father-heart. As the apostle Paul puts it, "You have received the spirit of sonship." So "we cry, 'Abba! Father!'" (Romans 8:15). John writes in his first letter that the unmistakable mark of a newborn babe in the family of God is that he immediately knows his Father, and calls Him Father (1 John 2:13).

What a far cry this is from some of the views of God that are abroad today. He is called The Ground of Being, The Ultimate Cause, The Infinite Mind, and on and on. It is true that God is all these things. They are not wrong but they are very inadequate. Paul, too, agrees that God is above all and through all and in all (Ephesians 4:6). He is the end and the beginning, the beginning and the end. All things exist because of Him, and all things lead back to Him.

But God is so much more than a remote Mind, the first Cause, an infinite Being. He is a Person, and He wants to know us and be known by us. He wants to have a deep, eternal fellowship with us. He wants us to have as intimate a relationship with Him as a child's relationship to an earthly father—in fact, much more so. Once you truly know God the Father as He desires to be known, you find that the only adequate way to address Him is "Father." No, not even Father, but *Abba!* which is an Aramaic word meaning literally, "Daddy" or "Da-da," the delighted, trusting sound a toddler makes when he's swept up in the arms of a proud, loving father. No other name expresses the intimate union with God a true Christian experiences.

That is why Jesus taught His disciples to pray, "Our Father, who art in heaven." That is why, as He knelt in the Garden of Gethsemane, in the very shadow of the cross, He called upon His Father, saying, "Abba, Father, . . . take away this cup from me; nevertheless not what I will, but what thou wilt" (Mark 14:36). That is why the apostle Paul tells us in two of his letters that the Spirit gives us the right to come before God, addressing Him even as Jesus did, "Abba! Father!" (see Romans 8:15; Galatians 4:6).

Internal and external unity

In these seven elements is found the nature of authentic Christian unity. It is not a union to be manufactured by our effort, but a unity that already exists, created in us, through us, and around us by the Spirit of God. These seven facets of unity are not, therefore, articles of theological agreement. They ought never to be put into a creedal statement as though agreement with these is what endorses someone as a Christian. No, it is the other way around: becoming a Christian ultimately brings agreement on these points. They are areas not just of doctrine, but of mutual experience. They are experiential truths that lay hold of us, not truths we are to lay hold of.

The seven elements of our unity are not debatable. If anyone challenges or disagrees with these, he is simply manifesting the fact that he is not yet a Christian. When he becomes a Christian he will experience and therefore understand these things. He may not be able to articulate them clearly but he will recognize them when they are described, for they are immediately experienced by all who are in Christ. Therefore, the way to create unity is simply to bring men and women to Christ. The unity of the Spirit will be produced in them by the Spirit. It is impossible to achieve any meaningful or significant union apart from this unity which is produced only by the Spirit.

Putting it in another way, there are two kinds of unity: an *external unity* without internal agreement, and an *internal unity* which manifests occasional external disagreement. We have been calling the first, union. The very nature of those who seek external union rather than true internal unity is to attempt to impose union by control and direction. These are the "control freaks" or "church bosses" who have to be at the top of the pyramid, imposing their vision of how their "Christian union" should function from the top down. Their power is measured by how successful they are in getting the conglomerate to follow them.

I remember well the first time I ran into the second kind of unity, the true, Spirit-created, internal kind of unity. As a boy I had two friends who were brothers, only a year apart in age. One day we were out playing and these brothers began quarreling. I thought that one was a bit sarcastic and unfair so I chimed in on behalf of the underdog. To my amazement he didn't welcome my help. In fact, he turned on me! And then his brother joined him, and *both* jumped on me!

I discovered I had made a very shallow judgment. I felt the differences they were airing represented a fundamental disagreement between them—but I was wrong! Underneath the disagreement was a fundamental unity: their brotherhood. The moment I attacked one of them, that unity manifested itself and they closed ranks against the outsider—me! This incident illustrates the unity of the church—an internal unity with an occasional external disagreement.

Now, as we apply this great central truth of Christian unity from Ephesians 4:4–6 to the outer areas of our lives—especially as we confront the problems of modern existence—it is clear that Christians are to direct their efforts not at producing an outward union but toward maintaining peace within the body. That is what Paul taught when he said to be "eager to maintain the unity of the Spirit in the bond of peace" (Ephesians 4:3). It is absolutely crucial that Christians practice Christlike love and put an end to quarreling, harboring grudges, and struggling against one another.

In John 17, Jesus said that our love and unity would be a witness to the world. He prayed that Christians "may all be one . . . that the world may believe that thou hast sent me" (verse 21). The degree to which division and hostility reign in the church is the degree to which that church's effectiveness will be hindered in its community. Our witness is neutralized by our unwillingness to maintain the unity which the Spirit has already given us. When we are divided, there is nothing we can say to which the world will pay any attention.

It is important that when Christians meet together

they realize that they are called to understand one another. They are to forbear one another, pray for one another, forgive one another, be kind and tender-hearted, not holding grudges, not being bitter, resentful, or hateful toward each other. This is where the Spirit aims when He comes among us. He moves toward the healing of resentment and the restoring of relationships.

This is how we maintain the unity that the Spirit has given us. We must get below the surface, behind the differences, so that the fundamental unity rises to the surface. We must recognize that our relationships are more important than the transitory issues that divide us. If the grace of God is truly at work in our lives, transforming our hearts, then the marvelous, underlying, fundamental unity that is there will come welling up, rising above all the differences and hurts, expressing itself by the Spirit of Jesus Christ, through acts of love manifested even to the unlovely.

Ephesians 4:4–6 also teaches that we cannot classify Christians by organizations. We cannot say that all Catholics are Christians or that all Baptists are believers (nor can we write people off because they are Catholics or Baptists!). We cannot maintain that all who belong to the Independent Fundamental Churches of America are Christians while all those who belong to the World Council of Churches are not. God's Spirit always over-leaps human boundaries. The unity of the Spirit will be found in people of many different groups, and we must recognize that fact. We shall find true Christians everywhere—and it becomes our responsibility to maintain the unity of the Spirit in the bond of peace wherever we find fellow believers in Christ.

Paul says in Romans 14, "As for the man who is weak in faith, welcome him, but not for disputes over opinions" (Romans 14:1). We are not to cast him out but to receive him. Receive him even though he does not see as clearly as you do and perhaps has not graduated from the right school. Nevertheless, receive him. Recognize him as a brother if he manifests love for Jesus Christ, no matter what his label may be.

Another lesson from this study is that true Christians may use the fact of basic internal unity to determine the area and kind of cooperation they can have with others, both Christian and non-Christian. After all, though we may not be one with everyone else as members of the body of Christ, we are one in sharing human life. We can join with anyone in the relief of human suffering, in establishing strong and just government, in the pursuit of better education and living conditions for our children, and in many other issues and enterprises in life. We are not to shut ourselves away from other human beings because they do not share the same life in Christ.

Opposite directions

But there is also an area where we can cooperate with some Christians who share the life of Jesus Christ, but cannot join with others. That area is in the enterprise of proclaiming the great life-changing message of the church, in evangelizing the world. The reason for this is that many who regard themselves as Christians have an understanding of the gospel that is entirely different from ours. What they are attempting to achieve is entirely different than what we seek to achieve. We and they go in opposite directions.

It is impossible, of course, to ride two horses going in opposite directions—to attempt it is to put a terrific strain upon the anatomy! The Israelites of old were taught this same truth when they were told not to yoke an ox and a donkey together (see Deuteronomy 22:10). Why not? Because they go at two different speeds and are two different heights. It would be cruel and counterproductive to link them together. They would simply chafe one another all the time. This is God's way of teaching symbolically that there are fundamental differences of gait and direction between people whose spiritual convictions are radically different. As Amos 3:3 tells us, two cannot walk together except they be agreed.

But someone may ask: "Can we worship together with others who do not share life in Jesus Christ?" The answer of the Bible is, clearly, *Yes*. God commands all people everywhere to worship Him (Psalm 66:1–2; Philippians 2:10–11). Wherever anyone is worshiping God as supreme and not some lesser concept of Him (as an idol) then Christians can join together with such in worship. The most elementary path for the approach of anyone to God is declared in Hebrews 11:6—"Whoever would draw near to God must believe that he exists and that he rewards those who seek him." Cornelius, the Roman centurion described in Acts 10, is an example of just such a person.

Having said all this, let us not forget the appeal of the apostle to the church to be faithful to its calling. The church does not have the right to chart its own course. Its purpose and goal have already been set, and even its function has been determined by its Lord. In the next section of Ephesians 4, the apostle turns to a detailed description of how the Lord has equipped His body to function effectively and with power in the world.

CHAPTER 4

ALL GOD'S CHILDREN HAVE GIFTS

Many people think that the incarnation of Jesus Christ began at the first Christmas and ended when Jesus was taken up into the clouds. But in fact, that was only the *beginning* of the incarnation of Christ. The process of the incarnation is still going on.

God's program for reaching and healing a broken world has always involved incarnation. The word *incarnate* means "to take bodily form." When God chose to demonstrate to humankind His love and the new life He offered us, He did so by incarnating Himself—by taking on our form, sharing our human experience, and living among us. God became flesh and dwelt among us. Jesus Christ was the incarnation of God, the God-man, God in human flesh.

But we make a great mistake if we think the incarnation ended with the earthly life of Christ. The life of Jesus is still being manifested upon the earth—but no longer through a single physical body, limited to one geographic location. Today, the body of Christ performs the work of Christ around the clock and around the globe. It is a corporate body, comprised of millions of individuals like you and me.

This body is called the church.

Open the book of Acts in the New Testament and you'll find that the writer of Acts, Dr. Luke, tells a certain young man named Theophilus that he had previously set down in his first account (the Gospel According to Luke) "all that Jesus *began* to do and teach." In Acts, the sequel to his gospel, Dr. Luke continues the record of Jesus' work among humankind—*yet Jesus Himself only appears in the first eleven verses of Acts!*

In verse 11, Jesus ascends into heaven. Yet the story of His work on earth continues for twenty-eight more chapters. How can that be? Because the rest of Acts is the story of the work of His *new* body, the church! When it lives in and by the Spirit, the church is nothing less than the physical extension of the life of Jesus to the whole world. The physical life of Jesus began at the moment a Jewish virgin named Mary conceived, and has continued without interruption right up to the moment you are reading this page—roughly two thousand years!

That is an amazing and all-important concept! What happened on a small scale in Judea and Galilee twenty centuries ago continues on a worldwide scale today, permeating every level of society and every aspect of human life. Once Christians discover and lay hold of this amazing truth for their own lives, their outlook on life is completely transformed. Their relationship with God becomes dynamic and exciting. Their lives become powerfully effective for God.

It is a thrilling adventure to rediscover the pattern by which God has designed His church to influence the world. On the other hand, there is nothing more pathetic and barren than a church that does not understand God's program for operating the body of Christ on earth. The church that fails to grasp this amazing concept is doomed to substitute business methods, organizational procedures, and pressure politics as means to influence society. Such a "church" is not really the church as God intended it to be; it is merely a religious extension of the dead systems of this world.

A new capacity for service

So let's examine and explore the amazing pattern of operation the apostle Paul describes as God's way of touching and changing the world. Let's look at God's "operating manual" for the new body of Christ on earth, the church. In Ephesians 4, Paul now turns from his description of the nature of the church to the provision made by the Holy Spirit for its dynamic, effective functioning in the world. He writes, "Grace was given to each of us according to the measure of Christ's gift" (Ephesians 4:7).

In that brief sentence there is a reference to two tremendous things: (1) the *gift of the Holy Spirit* for ministry, which is given to every true Christian without exception, and (2) the new and remarkable *power* by which that gift may be exercised. We will look carefully at both of these realities, but let us begin with the gift of the Spirit, which Paul refers to as a *grace*.

The word *grace* in the original language is *charis,* from which the English adjective, *charismatic*, is derived. This grace is a God-given capacity for service that we have received as Christians; we did not possess it before we became Christians. This grace is given to all true Christians, without exception.

Paul himself, in Ephesians 3:8, refers to one of his own gifts or graces of the Spirit: "To me, though I am the very least of all the saints, this grace [*charis*] was given." What was the grace? He goes on: "To preach to the Gentiles the unsearchable riches of Christ." Clearly one of his gifts was that of preaching—or, as it is called in other places, the gift of prophesying. When Paul writes to his young son in the faith, Timothy, he uses a closely related word when he says, "Hence I remind you to rekindle the gift [*charisma*] of God that is within you" (2 Timothy 1:6).

There seems little doubt that this is where the early church began with new converts. Whenever anyone, by faith in Jesus Christ, passed from the kingdom and power of Satan into the kingdom of God's love, he was immediately taught that the Holy Spirit of God had not only imparted to him the *life* of Jesus Christ, but had also equipped him with a *spiritual gift or gifts* which he was then responsible to discover and exercise. The apostle Peter writes, "As each has received a gift, employ it for one another, as good stewards of God's varied grace" (1 Peter 4:10). And again, in 1 Corinthians 12:7, Paul writes, "To each is given the manifestation of the Spirit for the common good."

It is significant that in each place where the gifts of the Spirit are described in Scripture, the emphasis is placed upon the fact that each Christian has at least one. That gift may be lying dormant within you, embryonic and unused. You may not know what it is, but it is there. The Holy Spirit makes no exceptions to this basic equipping of each believer. No Christian can say, "I can't serve God; I don't have any capacity or ability to serve Him." We have all, as authentic followers of Christ, been gifted with a "grace" of the Spirit.

It is vitally essential that you discover the gift or gifts you possess. The value of your life as a Christian will be determined by the degree to which you use the gift God has given you.

Varieties of gifts

The most detailed passage on the gifts of the Spirit is 1 Corinthians 12. There is another briefer list in Romans 12, and a still shorter list in 1 Peter 4. In these passages certain gifts are referred to by more than one name. By comparing the passages we can see that there are sixteen or seventeen basic gifts, and these may be found in various combinations within a single individual, each cluster of gifts opening the door to a wide and varied ministry.

Perhaps the most helpful way to become acquainted with these gifts is to allow the apostle Paul to teach us about them from the great explanation he gives to the church at Corinth: "Now there are varieties of gifts, but the same Spirit; and there are varieties of service, but the same Lord; and there are varieties of working, but it is the same God who inspires them all in every one" (1 Corinthians 12:4–6).

Notice the three divisions of the subject of spiritual gifts. There are *gifts*; there are *ministries* (called *service* here); and there are *workings* (or *energizings*). Gifts are linked to the Spirit, ministries are linked to the Lord Jesus, and workings are linked to God the Father. Thus, as in Ephesians 4, the triune God is seen dwelling within His body, the church, for the specific purpose of ministering to a broken world (see Ephesians 4:3–6).

A *gift*, as we have already seen, is a specific capacity or function which is given to us directly by the Spirit of God. This is critically important to understand. We do not generate these gifts ourselves; they are implanted in us by the Spirit Himself. Because we have been gifted by God, we can think *highly enough* of ourselves to have confidence in carrying out the ministry He has given us. We know we can accomplish His will, because He has given us the spiritual ability to do so.

But we also know we should not think *too highly* of ourselves, because the Spirit of God is the source of the gifts, not we ourselves. Properly viewed, spiritual gifts elevate us and keep us humble at the same time!

A *ministry* is the sphere in which a gift is performed, among a certain group of people, or in a certain geographic area. It is the sovereign right and prerogative of the Lord Jesus to assign a sphere of service for each member of His body. You can see Him exercising that right in the John 21. There, after His resurrection, He appears to Peter and three times bids him, "Feed my sheep." That was to be Peter's ministry. He was to be a pastor (or elder), feeding the flock of God. (Peter refers to himself in this capacity in 1 Peter 5.) When Peter expresses curiosity as to what the Lord would have John do, the Lord says to him, "What is that to you? Follow me!" (see John 21:15–23).

The Lord is still exercising this right today. He sets some to the task of teaching Christians. He sends others to minister to the "worldlings," those who are outside of the church. To some He gives the task of training youth and to others a ministry to older people. Some work with women and others with men; some go to the Jews, others to the Gentiles. Peter was sent to the circumcised (the Jews), while Paul was sent to the uncircumcised (the Gentiles). They both had the same gift, but their ministry was different.

Then there are *workings*, or energizings. These are the responsibility of the Father. The term refers to the degree of power by which a gift is manifested or ministered on a specific occasion. There are varieties of workings, the apostle says, but it is the same God who inspires them all in everyone (1 Corinthians 12:6).

Every exercise of a spiritual gift does not produce the same result each time. The same message given in several different circumstances will not produce the same results. What is the difference? It is God's choice. He is endlessly creative and does not intend to produce the same results every time. He could, but He does not always desire to do so. It is up to the Father to determine how much is accomplished at each ministry of a gift.

The Scriptures record that John the Baptist did no miracle throughout the course of his ministry. Yet he was a mighty prophet of God, and Jesus said of him that there is no man born of woman who is greater than he (see Matthew 11:11). There are those today who suggest that if we cannot do miracles it is a sign of weakness in faith and of little spiritual power. But John did no miracles. Why not? Because there are varieties of workings, and it was not the choice of the Father to work through John in that way.

Twin gifts

Now, in 1 Corinthians 12, we come to the list of specific spiritual gifts: "To one is given through the

Spirit the utterance of wisdom, and to another the utterance of knowledge according to the same Spirit. . . ." (verse 8).

Here is a pair of gifts: the gift of wisdom and the gift of knowledge. These often appear together in a single individual, for they are related to the same function. They are concerned with *utterance*—or as it is in the original, *the word*. The gift of knowledge is the ability to perceive and systematize the great facts God has hidden in His Word. A person exercising this gift is able to recognize the key and important facts of Scripture as a result of investigation. The gift of wisdom, on the other hand, is the ability to apply those insights to a specific situation. It is wisdom that puts knowledge to work.

Perhaps you have been in a meeting where some problem was being discussed and there is a seeming impasse—no one seems to know what to do or what the answer is. Then someone stands up and takes some great principle of Scripture and applies it to the problem in such a clear way that everyone can see the answer. That is the gift of wisdom being exercised.

These twin gifts of wisdom and knowledge are also related to the gift of teaching, which is explored in chapter 11. Teaching deals with communication. It is the ability to impart the facts and insights which the gifts of knowledge and wisdom discover, and to pass them on to others in learnable form. The man or woman who possesses all three of these gifts is a valuable person to have around indeed!

Then Paul mentions the gift of faith. This faith is again different from what we discussed in chapter 3. All Christians have faith; faith is the prerequisite to salvation. But some Christians have the gift or "grace" of faith. What Paul means here is essentially what we call today the gift of vision. It is the ability to see something that needs to be done and to believe that God will do it even though it looks impossible. Trusting that sense of faith, a person with this gift moves out and accomplishes the "impossible" task in God's name. Every great Christian enterprise has begun with a man or woman who possessed the gift of faith.

Some years ago, in the Taiwan Republic of China, I met a remarkable woman named Lillian Dickson. Clearly and unmistakably, Mrs. Dickson had the gift of faith. When she saw a need, she moved right in to meet it, regardless of whether she could see an adequate supply of funds or resources. She became concerned about certain poor boys on the streets of Taipei who had no homes. They were orphans, cast adrift by their families. Her heart went out to them because of the pressures that forced them into a life of crime. Because she had the gift of faith and a clear vision of what God could do, she started an organization to rescue those boys. From all around the world, God moved people to send her money for that project and many others which she ran. As a result of this one woman's faith and vision, the lives of hundreds of Chinese street boys were transformed. That's the gift of faith in action.

Healing at every level

Next the apostle mentions "gifts of healing" given by the same Spirit. That word in the original Greek is in the plural form: "healings." I take that to mean healing at every level of human need—physical, emotional, and spiritual.

In the early church there were a number of instances where this gift was exercised on the physical level. Throughout church history there have been others who had this gift of physical healing. There are some today who call themselves "healers," but it should be noted that none of the apostles ever made this claim for themselves. However, there is abundant evidence in the New Testament that the Spirit of God worked through the apostles and other believers in bringing physical healing to the sick, just as He does today.

Some claims to healing today are based on spectacular but temporary improvement as a result of strong psychological conditioning, and the healing fades away within a few days. But God does heal today, sometimes quickly and permanently; this fact is too well attested and documented to challenge. We only note here that such healing does not necessarily indicate that the gift of healing is being exercised.

If someone asks, "Why is this gift so infrequently manifested today?" the answer is given in 1 Corinthians 12:11—"All these are inspired by one and the same Spirit, who apportions to each one individually as he wills." The spiritual gift of physical healing is not seen often today because it is apparently not the will of the Spirit for it to be given in these days as widely as it was in the early church.

The gift of healing is, however, frequently bestowed today on the emotional and spiritual level. Many Christians, laymen and professional ministers alike, are equipped by the Spirit to help those with damaged emotions and with bruised spirits, who have become sick or disordered in these areas. They make excellent counselors because they are able to exercise the patience and compassion necessary to help such wounded souls.

The purpose of miracles

Along with the gift of healing is the gift of miracles. This is the ability to short-circuit the processes of nature by supernatural activity, as the Lord did when He turned water into wine or multiplied the loaves and fishes. Some may have this gift today. I don't doubt that it can be given.

The gifts of physical healing and miracles are given for the initial building up of faith, as a bridge to move Christians from dependence upon things they can see to faith in a God who can work and accomplish much when nothing seems to be happening. The history of missions will substantiate this. So does the flow of the book of Acts: In the beginning of Acts, we see a number of miraculous events being worked by various apostles. But as the church grows and is established in the faith, the miraculous events of the book of Acts taper off. The implications of this flow of events are clear: God wants us to walk by faith, not by sight. As faith grows, we have less need of visible demonstrations of God's power. He wants us to become mature enough that the "battery" of our faith no longer needs to be repeatedly "jump-started" by miracles.

The apostle goes on to mention the gift of prophecy. This is the greatest gift of all, as Paul makes clear by devoting an entire chapter—1 Corinthians 14—to this gift. We shall examine the gift of prophecy more fully when we return to Ephesians 4 and the ministry of the prophet. But here, in 1 Corinthians 14:3, the apostle says of this gift, "On the other hand, he who prophesies speaks to men for their upbuilding and encouragement and consolation." That is the effect of the gift of prophecy. When a man or woman has this gift it results in building, stimulating, and encouraging others. This is not a gift for preachers only. All the gifts are given without respect to a person's theological training or vocational calling. Many laymen and laywomen have the gift of prophecy and should be exercising it.

Then there is the gift of discernment of spirits. This is the ability to distinguish between the spirit of error and the spirit of truth before the difference is manifest to all by the results. It is the ability to see through a phony before his phoniness is clearly evident. When Ananias and Sapphira came to Peter, bringing what they claimed to be the full price of some land they had sold though they had actually kept back part of it for themselves, Peter exercised the gift of discernment when he said, "How is it that you have agreed together to tempt the Spirit of the Lord? You have not lied to men but to God" (Acts 5:4, 9). Those who have this gift can read a book and sense the subtlety of error in it, or hear a message and put their finger on what may be wrong about it. It is a valuable gift to be exercised within the church.

Another pair of gifts is listed next: tongues and the interpretation of tongues. From time to time there is a resurgence of interest in these gifts. All such movements must be examined in the light of the Scriptures. Does the expression of these gifts glorify Christ? Is there ample biblical authority for the teachings of those who practice these gifts? Do these gifts promote unity in the body of Christ? Are those who practice these gifts characterized by Christlike holiness, humility, and love? Do they bring permanent improvement to the individual and to the church?

These are the questions that must be answered

affirmatively to verify and validate the expression of these gifts.

Distinctive marks

In Scripture, the gift of tongues always had at least three distinctive marks which are clearly described in the New Testament. First, as on the day of Pentecost, the gift of tongues consisted of known languages which were spoken somewhere on earth (see Acts 2:1–13). The description "unknown tongue" that appears in the King James Version has no support in the original Greek text. The tongues of the New Testament were not a torrent of unrelated syllables; they had structure and syntax, as any earthly language has.

Second, the biblical gift was characterized by praise and thanksgiving addressed to God. Paul wrote, "For one who speaks in a tongue speaks not to men but to God" (1 Corinthians 14:2). The gift of tongues is definitely not a means of preaching the gospel or of conveying messages to groups or individuals, but is—as it was on the day of Pentecost—a means of praising God for His mighty works.

Third, the gift of tongues was intended as a sign to unbelievers and not as a sign for believers. Paul is very precise about this. He quotes the prophet Isaiah as having predicted the purpose of tongues: "In the law it is written, 'By men of strange tongues and by the lips of foreigners will I speak to this people, and even then they will not listen to me, says the Lord.' Thus, tongues are a sign not for believers but for unbelievers, while prophecy is not for unbelievers but for believers" (1 Corinthians 14:21–22).

The appearance of this gift at Pentecost marked the fact that God was judging the nation Israel and turning from it to the Gentiles (see Acts 2:1–13). This is why Peter said to the Jews on the Day of Pentecost, "For the promise is to you and to your children [the Jews] and to all that are far off [Gentiles], every one whom the Lord our God calls to him" (Acts 2:39).

Although it is not explicitly stated in Scripture as a distinguishing characteristic, it is nevertheless a striking fact that the biblical gift of tongues was everywhere publicly exercised and was evidently not intended for private use. We are told that the gifts of the Spirit are for the common good, and not for personal benefit. Each occasion with which tongues is connected in the New Testament was a public meeting. The setting for 1 Corinthians 14 is the assembly of Christians together for mutual ministry and worship.

When a Christian exercised the gift in prayer and thanksgiving to God it was valueless to the church unless it was interpreted. And Paul forbids its exercise in church unless there is definite assurance of interpretation for the edification of those present.

Since the gift of tongues is the easiest of the gifts to counterfeit, there have been imitations of it through the centuries. Whether those manifestations are the true gift or not can only be determined by their agreement with the biblical distinctives. We should remember that the primary purpose of *any* gift of the Spirit is to minister to the body of Christ, to edify and strengthen the body, and to accomplish the specific aim of the Holy Spirit in giving the gift.

Gifted to help

At the close of 1 Corinthians 12 there is another list of spiritual gifts, some of which duplicate the gifts already discussed: "God has appointed in the church first apostles, second prophets, third teachers, then workers of miracles, then healers, helpers, administrators, speakers in various kinds of tongues" (verse 28).

We shall reserve the consideration of apostles, prophets, and teachers till a later chapter, for these belong to a special class of gifts. The gifts of miracles and of healings we have already looked at, but a wonderful gift is mentioned here for the first time: the gift of helps. In some ways this is one of the greatest gifts, and it is certainly the most widespread. This gift is the ability to lend a hand wherever a need appears, and to do so in such a way as to strengthen, support, and encourage others.

In the church, the gift of helps is often manifest in those who serve as ushers and treasurers, in those who prepare the communion table or arrange flowers and serve dinners. The gift of helps is not a flashy gift, and many people with this all-important gift function in obscurity and anonymity—but God sees and knows the contribution of these humble, helping servants. More than most people realize, the exercise of this gift makes possible the ministry of the other, more evident, gifts. Every church is deeply indebted to those who exercise the gift of helps.

Exhorting, giving, leading

In the twelfth chapter of Romans is another partial treatment of spiritual gifts: "Having gifts that differ according to the grace given to us, let us use them. If prophecy, in proportion to our faith; if service, in our serving; he who teaches, in his teaching; he who exhorts, in his exhortation; he who contributes, in liberality; he who gives aid, with zeal; he who does acts of mercy, with cheerfulness" (verses 6–8).

We have already touched briefly upon the gift of prophecy and shall study it further when we return to Ephesians 4. The gift of serving seems to be identical with the gift of helps just examined. The word for "serving" is the same Greek word from which the word *deacon* comes. A deacon, then, would be anyone who uses the gift of helps to perform a service on behalf of, or in the name of, the church.

The gift of teaching we have already discussed as having to do with the realm of communication of truth. The next gift in this list is that of *exhortation*. This is a word that means to encourage or comfort another. Its Greek root means "to call alongside" and gives us the picture of someone calling another to come alongside for strengthening or reassurance. It is the same root from which a name of the Holy Spirit is derived: the *Comforter*, or in the RSV, the *Counselor*. Those who have this gift are able to inspire others to action, awaken renewed spiritual interest, or steady those who are struggling, stressed, or faltering.

Another gift mentioned for the first time here is that of contributing, or of giving. This gift is essentially concerned with the giving of money, so Paul's exhortation is that those with the gift of giving should do so with generosity. It may surprise many to learn that the Holy Spirit gives such a gift as this, but many Christians possess it, both the wealthy and the poor. It is the ability to earn and give money for the advancement of God's work, and to do so with such wisdom, humility, and cheerfulness that the recipients are immeasurably strengthened and blessed by the transaction.

A person with the gift of giving does not give with the idea of getting back or of using his donation as leverage to control the use of the gift or other aspects of the church's agenda. I have often had the experience of Christians coming to me with an offer to finance a certain ministry at considerable, sacrificial cost to themselves. They do so because they have the gift of giving, because it is their joy and reward to give, and because they seek the commendation of their Lord: "Well done, good and faithful servant."

The next gift listed by Paul is widely misunderstood because it is poorly translated. The Revised Standard Version says that the Christian who "gives aid" is to do it with zeal. Phillips is closer to the sense of the original: "Let the man who wields authority think of his responsibility." And the New English Bible is right on, rendering this phrase, "If you are a leader, exert yourself to lead." This might best be called the gift of leadership. The Greek word literally means, "one who stands in front." It is clearly evidenced in facilitating meetings, conducting seminars and panel discussions, chairing boards and organizations, and the like, and it speaks to the fact that those who exercise the leadership function should do so in a way that edifies and helps others spiritually.

The final gift mentioned in Romans 12 is that of doing acts of mercy. Its distinctiveness is indicated by the meaning of the word *mercy*. Mercy is undeserved aid, aid given to those who most people find repugnant and offensive—the sick and deformed, the unwashed and foul, those with unpleasant personalities and vile habits. It differs from the gift of helps by being directed to those who are either undeserving or who (like a child with AIDS or a mentally disordered individual) is an innocent victim, treated as an outcast by much of our society.

I have seen many people at Peninsula Bible Church who have this gift, and they use it to work among retarded children, or in the AIDS ward of Bay Area hospitals, or in prison visitation ministries, or in service to the homeless and the immigrant poor, or in twelve-step ministries to alcoholics and drug addicts. The love and patience exhibited by those with the gift of mercy is beautiful to watch.

These, then, are the "graces" that are distributed by the Holy Spirit to each member of the body of Christ as the Spirit chooses. There are no exceptions, and no one is left out. This is the fundamental provision of the Lord for the operation of His church. As a physical human body consists of numerous cells exercising various functions, so the body of Christ consists of many members, each possessing a specific function that is absolutely essential to the effective, healthy functioning of the body.

It is obvious that there can be no hope of ever getting the church to operate as it was intended to until each individual member recognizes and begins to exercise the spiritual gifts he or she has received. So fundamentally important is this issue that we shall take an extra chapter to look at the gifts from a wider point of view. In the next chapter, we will examine practical ways to discover and use your spiritual gifts.

CHAPTER 5

DISCOVERING AND USING YOUR GIFT

You are unique, unreproducible, and irreplaceable. In all the universe, there is no one who looks exactly like you, thinks your thoughts, or feels your feelings. Above all, there is no other Christian in the world who is equipped and gifted like you. Within you, permeating your being, is a uniquely designed pattern of spiritual gifts. The body of Christ needs you and the gifts the Spirit has uniquely bestowed upon you.

The church is primarily and fundamentally a body designed to express through each unique, individual member the life of the indwelling Lord. Every member of the body is equipped by the Holy Spirit with gifts designed to express that life. Once you become fully aware that God Himself has uniquely equipped you with spiritual gifts, and that He has strategically placed you exactly where He wants you in order to use those gifts, then you enter a whole new dimension of exciting possibilities! In all the world there is no experience more satisfying and fulfilling than to realize that you have been the instrument of the divine plan which God is working out in the world, in human history, and in the lives of the people around you. Such an experience awaits any true Christian who is willing to discover and use the spiritual gifts God has given.

Discovering our spiritual gifts is not something we do by taking a self-test, like one of those true-or-false quizzes in a magazine. It takes time. It takes thought. It takes Scripture study. It takes interaction with other Christians. Above all, it requires that we submit ourselves to the authority of the Head of the body, Jesus Christ, who reserves to Himself the right to coordinate and direct its activities.

The deepest level

One common area of confusion—and one fact we must clearly understand—is that a spiritual gift is *not* the same as a natural talent. It is true that talents such as musical ability, artistic skills, athletic coordination, and the like are also gifts from God. But they are not *spiritual* gifts. They are gifts on a physical or social level only, given to benefit people in the natural realm.

Spiritual gifts, on the other hand, are given to benefit people and the church in the realm of the Spirit, the realm of an individual's relationship to God. The effect of a spiritual gift is to enhance a person in his own spirit's enjoyment of the life and love of God—to bless him, in other words. Moreover, since the spirit is the most fundamental part of person's being, from which all other relationships flow, it is clear that the exercise of spiritual gifts operates at the deepest level of human existence, and strikes right at the root of all human problems.

Talents deal more with the surfaces of life. Though useful or entertaining, talents do not permanently affect and change people as spiritual gifts can do. Talents, obviously, are distributed to men and women quite apart from any reference to their spiritual condition. Non-Christians as well as Christians have talents, and both can find many opportunities for useful expression of their talents in both religious and secular settings. Only Christians have spiritual gifts, because these gifts are given only to those in whom the Spirit of Christ has come to dwell (1 Corinthians 12:7).

It is quite possible, therefore, for a Christian to have a talent for teaching, for instance, but not to have the spiritual gift of teaching. If that is the case and he were asked to teach a Sunday School class, for example, he would be quite capable of imparting considerable information and knowledge of facts to his class—but his teaching would lack the power to bless and advance his students spiritually. This fact helps to explain the many qualified secular teachers who do not do well at all as Sunday school teachers. On the other hand, many school teachers also possess, as Christians, the spiritual gift of teaching and are greatly used of God in Bible classes and Sunday school teaching.

It is also quite possible to exercise a spiritual gift through the channel of a natural talent. This is frequently seen in the ministry of Christian singers. We have all heard Christian soloists with great voices whose musical talents would have pleased secular audiences anywhere. But in addition to their talent, they possessed great power to impart spiritual enrichment through their singing, leaving their audiences spiritually refreshed and strengthened. Most often it is the gift of exhortation that the singer is exercising, but it is being carried by his or her musical talent just as a telephone wire carries a human voice.

Of course we have all been treated also to the disappointing experience of listening to a Christian performer sing without exercising any spiritual gift. It may have been a virtuoso performance, a triumph of technical artistry, yet we find our hearts are left cold and unmoved. The lesson is clear: Don't try to use your natural talents *alone* to accomplish the work of God, for talent alone cannot operate in that sphere. But if you use your talents as channels or vehicles for your spiritual gifts, then you will find they dovetail beautifully, just as you might expect they would since both talents and gifts come from the same God.

Perhaps the question most pressing upon you right now is, "How do I discover my spiritual gifts? If they are the doorway to a new world of fulfillment and challenge, then I surely want to know what mine are! But where do I begin to discover them?" The answer is really very simple. You discover a spiritual gift just like you discovered your natural talents!

A special appeal

How did you find out that you were musically talented? Or artistically endowed? Or able to lead, to organize, or to compete athletically? It probably first began with some kind of desire. You simply liked whatever it is you are talented at, and found yourself drawn toward those who were already doing it. You enjoyed watching those who were good at it, and came to appreciate something of the fine points of the activity. That is the way spiritual gifts make themselves known at first too.

Many Christians today have somehow gotten the idea that doing what God wants you to do is always dreary and unpleasant, that Christians must always make choices between doing what they want to do and being happy on the one hand, versus doing what God wants them to do and being completely miserable on the other. Nothing could be further from the truth.

The exercise of a spiritual gift is always a satisfying, enjoyable experience though sometimes the occasion on which it is exercised may be an unhappy one. Jesus said it was His constant delight to do the will of the One who sent Him. The Father's gift awakened His own desire, and He went about doing what He intensely enjoyed doing.

Here is a practical, step-by-step plan for discovering your spiritual gifts:

1. Start with the gifts you most feel drawn toward. Study the biblical lists of gifts and try exercising those gifts that most appeal to you.

2. Watch for improvement and development. Do you get better at it as you go along? Do you find your quite understandable initial fears subsiding and a growing sense of competence developing? Remember, that's the way it was in discovering your talents, too.

3. Ask trusted Christian friends to observe your life and tell you what gifts they see in you. Often, others can see our lives more clearly than we can, and they can help to affirm gifts in us that we cannot clearly see as yet. (The mutual affirming of spiritual gifts is one of the many benefits Christians gain when they are close *koinonia*-fellowship and community with one another.)

In fact, the observation of other Christians provide us with a good "reality check" for our spiritual gifts. Many Christians wonder, "Do I have a certain spiritual gift, or don't I?" Here's a final test: Do others recognize this gift in you? When someone says to you, quite unsolicited, "We'd like you to take on this ministry, we think you have a gift for it," then you can be reasonably sure you have that spiritual gift. It may well be that others will see that gift in you long before you do!

One of the best things you can do for another Christian—and for the life of the body as a whole—is to help another Christian discover his or her spiritual gifts. It is much better for others to affirm authentic gifts in you than for you to lay a pretentious claim on gifts you might not actually have! One great Bible teacher used to say, "It's such a pity to see someone who thinks he has the gift of preaching—but no one in his congregation has the gift of listening!"

Gifts need to be exercised just as talents do. Practice tends to make perfect, whether in the use of talents or the use of gifts. As Paul wrote to young Timothy, "Rekindle the gift of God that is within you" (2 Timothy 1:6). As your skill in the exercise of a gift develops, the spiritual blessing it brings will become increasingly evident. You will find yourself seeking more and more occasions to use your gift. But remember: that gift was not given to you for your own personal, worldly advancement, but as a means to spiritually enrich yourself and others. As Paul reminds us, "To each is given the manifestation of the Spirit for the common good" (1 Corinthians 12:7).

It is helpful, also, to realize that hardly anyone discovers all his gifts at the beginning of his Christian experience. Gifts, like talents, may lie undiscovered for years, then emerge when a certain combination of needs or circumstances brings them to light. It is wise, therefore, to always be ready to try something new. Who knows but what the Spirit of God has put you on the doorstep of a new endeavor for the express purpose of helping you discover gifts you never knew you had!

Should we seek specific gifts?

Many Christians wonder, "Is it proper to pray for a certain specific gift to be given me?" Bible teachers differ on the answer to this one. Some feel that the pattern of gifts you possess are all determined by the Spirit at the moment He takes up residence within you. It may take you years to discover your gifts, but they are all there from the beginning, from the moment of your salvation, and no new ones are ever added.

Others point to the verse which says, "But earnestly desire the higher gifts" (1 Corinthians 12:31), and feel that the Bible encourages prayer for specific gifts. It should be noted that this exhortation is in the plural and is closer to a Southern "y'all" than to a singular "you." Thus the apostle wanted these Corinthian believers to pray that God would manifest the best gifts in their midst by sending among them individuals equipped with these gifts; it was not meant for individual encouragement to seek specific gifts.

However, in 1 Corinthians 14:13, Paul does say, "He who speaks in a tongue should pray for the power to interpret." Whatever else is meant by these verses, it is clear that certain gifts are more useful and profitable than others, and every church is to be concerned that the best ones are in evidence in their midst. Certainly the final choice is left to the Spirit, for Paul says that the Spirit "apportions to each one individually as he wills" (1 Corinthians 12:11). Hebrews 2:4 also speaks of "gifts of the Holy Spirit distributed according to his own will."

Infinite variety

In the preceding chapter we mentioned the fact that the gifts, though only about seventeen or eighteen in number, are given in clusters or combinations that make possible an almost infinite number of varying ministries. Someone once computed the number of potential combinations or permutations that this number of gifts makes possible, and the number has so many digits it is impossible for me to comprehend!

Every human face is made up of the same basic components—a pair of eyes, a nose, a mouth, two cheeks, a chin, a forehead, all held in by a pair of ears. Yet no two faces in the world are exactly alike. In the same way, no two Christians have exactly the same pattern of spiritual gifts. God gave you your face because it is exactly right for the expression of His life where you are. Likewise He gives you the precise combination of gifts you possess because that combination is exactly what is needed for the Lord's ministry. Be open to His leading, and He will show you where and how He wants you to use your gifts.

Do you see what this means? It completely eliminates competition within the body of Christ! No Christian needs to be the rival of any other; there is a place for all in the body, and no one can take another Christian's place.

In fact, Paul goes on to say as much in the latter half of 1 Corinthians 12. There are two attitudes, he says, that are completely eliminated by the existence of spiritual gifts. One is self-depreciation:

"If the foot should say, 'Because I am not a hand, I do not belong to the body,' that would not make it any less a part of the body. And if the ear should say, 'Because I am not an eye, I do not belong to the body,' that would not make it any less a part of the body" (1 Corinthians 12:15–16).

This completely destroys the argument of the Christian who says, "There's nothing I can do; others have gifts and abilities but since I can't do what they do I must not be of much use in the church." Paul's conclusion to this line of argument is: "But as it is, God arranged the organs in the body, each one of them, as he chose" (verse 18).

On the other hand, there is no room for arrogance or self-sufficiency either:

> The eye cannot say to the hand, 'I have no need of you,' nor again the head to the feet, 'I have no need of you.' On the contrary, the parts of the body which seem to be weaker are indispensable, and those parts of the body which we think less honorable we invest with the greater honor, and our unpresentable parts are treated with greater modesty, which our more presentable parts do not require (verses 21–24).

No member of the body has the right to look down on the ministry of another Christian. We desperately need each other in the body of Christ. No Christian, or group of Christians, can do the task alone. No denomination constitutes the whole body, and no Christian organization possesses all the gifts in the variety of combinations necessary to do the work God wants done today. We are members one of another, and it is time we took these words seriously and began to act like one harmonious body again.

His body in the world

The gifts of the Spirit are not only for use within the church. They are for the world as well. Some who have the gift of teaching ought to be exercising it in their homes. Some who have the gift of helping ought to be using it in the office, the shop, or wherever they are. Some who have the gift of wisdom should be putting it to work wherever they touch people. These gifts are intended for all of life.

Remember that the ministry of the body is the ministry of Jesus Christ, His continuing ministry in human society. Christ loves this world and the men and women in it. He loves the homeless, the alcoholics, the sexaholics, the prostitutes, the gang members and graffiti taggers, the down-and-outers on Crack Street, the up-and-outers on Park Avenue, the Generation Xers who have given up on the future, the Baby Boomers who have achieved their career goals and status goals and still feel hollow inside. Jesus loves them all, and He wants to reach them and enfold them into His body.

Our job is to go to them, tell them about the Savior who has given His life for them, the Father who gave His only Son for them, and the Spirit who wants to empower them and indwell them. Our job is to exercise our gifts in order to urge, draw, and love people into the kingdom of God and the body of Christ. That is why God has equipped us with gifts, and filled us with His life. As we discover and use the gifts He has given us, we become His hands, His mouth, His feet, going out into the world, telling His story, doing His work, sharing His love, completing His eternal plan for the redemption of this broken world!

CHAPTER 6

ACCORDING TO THE POWER

Pastor Johnson leaned against the fender of the fire truck, watching helplessly as the church building burned to the ground. The firefighters continued battling the flames, but it was clear that the flames were winning. Just then, Mrs. Wimple, one of Pastor Johnson's Easter-only parishioners, came up to him, shaking her head sadly. "Oh, Pastor Johnson," she said sympathetically, "it's just awful! It doesn't look like they'll be able to save any of it!"

"No," Pastor Johnson sighed. "It's a total loss for sure. By the way, Mrs. Wimple, I usually only see you at church once a year! What brings you out here tonight?"

"Well," she said, spreading her hands, "this is the first time I've ever seen the church on fire!"

In this chapter, we will look at how to set a church "on fire" all year round, so that it will illuminate the world and draw people out of their darkness toward the light of Jesus Christ. An "on-fire" church is a church that is plugged into a source of power. What is that power source? And how does an "on-fire," fully powered church function? Is it a place where dramatic miracles happen every Sunday? Is it a center of political pressure, changing society by the power of its numbers, marching in lock-step? Is it a center of political activism, demanding change through protests and marches? Is it a religious think-tank, performing studies and issuing papers and resolutions in the hope that society will listen and change?

The apostle Paul, in his letter to the Ephesians, talks a lot about the power that resides in the church—yet he never mentions any of these activities. Instead, he reminds us that the fundamental secret of the operation of the church is that each true Christian has a gift and is expected to operate that gift or cluster of gifts in the power provided by Jesus Christ. This is the way he puts it:

"But grace was given to each of us according to the measure of Christ's gift. Therefore it is said, 'When he ascended on high he led a host of captives, and he gave gifts to men.' (In saying, 'He ascended,' what does it mean but that he had also descended into the lower parts of the earth? He who descended is he who also ascended far above all the heavens, that he might fill all things)" (4:7–10).

Now, there are two kinds of gifts mentioned in verse 7. Paul calls one the measure of the other: "But grace [that is the first gift] was given to each of us, according to the measure of Christ's gift" (or more literally, the gift of Christ—the second gift). This "gift of Christ" is the more basic gift of the two and refers to Christ Himself. Paul is not talking here about something Christ gives to us, but something God gives to us, which is Christ. The gift is Christ Himself. As Paul says in 2 Corinthians 9:15, "Thanks be to God for his inexpressible gift!"

Because Christ is made known to us by the presence of the Holy Spirit in our lives, it is equally proper to call this the gift of the Holy Spirit, as the apostle Peter does in Acts 2:38: "Peter said to them, 'Repent, and be baptized every one of you in the name of Jesus Christ for the forgiveness of your sins; and you shall receive the gift of the Holy Spirit.' "

So the basic gift is the indwelling of the Spirit of Christ within each believer. That is what makes anyone a Christian. Paul says to the Romans, "Anyone who does not have the Spirit of Christ does not belong to him" (Romans 8:9). He may be religious and a member of a local church, faithfully attending all meetings and fulfilling all obligations, but if he does not have the Spirit living within he is not one of Christ's. That is the essential requirement.

There is also the special "grace" mentioned here which is the gift of the Spirit to each Christian as a special ability or capacity for service. We have examined these in detail. It is this gift (or cluster of gifts) that must be exercised "according to the measure of Christ's gift."

Christ's triumphal march

In Ephesians 4:8–10, the apostle ties the *gift* of Christ to the *ascension* of Christ and His previous descent to earth. He writes, "Therefore it is said, 'When he ascended on high he led a host of captives, and he gave gifts to men.'" There, Paul quotes Psalm 68:18, then he continues, "(In saying, 'He ascended,' what does it mean but that he had also descended into the lower parts of the earth? He who descended is he who also ascended far above all the heavens, that he might fill all things)." In this passage, Paul seems to put great emphasis on Christ's triumphal march, leading a host of captives into heaven. What is Paul saying?

It is obvious that the quotation from Psalm 68 is intended to amplify and explain the phrase, "according to the measure of the gift of Christ." A gift is one thing, the power to use it is quite another. Paul is bringing the gift and the power together. Graces or gifts, he says, are given to us to use according to the measure of power available to us. And that power is the life of a risen and enthroned Lord, living within us by means of His Spirit.

Now we have to ask ourselves, "What kind of power do we need to operate the gifts God has given us?" Some people think we need the power of a strong personality in order to use our spiritual gifts. Many Christians who do not have a strong personality—who are shy or quiet by nature—neglect the gifts God has given them because they think, "Oh, I wish I had an extroverted personality so God could use me, but I'm just not outgoing enough to exercise spiritual gifts." But if the power we need to use our spiritual gifts is the power of an outgoing personality, then clearly there are many who will never have a chance to serve God with their gifts!

Well, is it the power of positive thinking that is required? We read much about this "power" today. Motivational books, tapes, infomercials, and seminars have never been more popular than they are today. Do we need to develop and energize our inner attitudes in such a way that we are always thinking positively so that we can become useful to Jesus Christ? If that is the kind of "power" we need, then it is clear we cannot be useful to God if we are sad, grieving, depressed, or suffering—and that is simply not true! The fact is, positive thinking is nothing more than wishful thinking if the facts of a situation are contrary to what we desire. While it's good to be optimistic, our optimism must be rooted in truth in order to be of any use at all.

Well, then, maybe the "power" we need to exercise spiritual gifts is the power of a keen intellect. If we have a well-trained, well-educated mind, honed to the highest degree by the resources of modern knowledge, then we will be empowered to use our spiritual gifts, right? If that's true, then what about all the people who have a limited IQ or limited education? Has God shut them out of being able to access the gifts and graces of the Spirit of God? Preposterous! The biblical teaching on spiritual gifts makes it clear that these gifts are for everyone in the body of Christ, not just an elite few.

Clearly, the power to exercise our spiritual gifts must be a different kind of power than any of the "powers" we have just examined. It *must* be a power that is superior to all circumstances. We need a kind of power that is not dependent upon personality, emotions, moods, intelligence, or education. We need a kind of power that is available to all Christians, in all circumstances, at all times.

That is precisely the kind of power the apostle Paul refers to when he speaks of the ascension and triumphal appearance of Christ before the throne of God that He might give gifts to people. It is the power of a risen Lord, the power of resurrection! Paul deeply desired this kind of power for himself. As he cries out in his Philippian letter, "that I may know him and the power of his resurrection" (Philippians 3:10). Because of the descent of Christ to earth (His incarnation), and His ascent again to the throne of power after His resurrection, that remarkable power is now available to *all* Christians!

It took His descent from glory down to this earth—with all the pain and anguish of the cross, plus His resurrection from the dead and His an ascension in triumph to receive gifts from the Father—before it was possible for Him to give those gifts to you. Remember, a spiritual gift is no common thing. As we have seen, it is not merely a natural talent. It is divinely given ability requiring resurrection power to exercise it. The gifts, therefore, which Christ has given you are the most precious gifts you could ever have.

Plugged into the source

Spiritual gifts can be compared to electrical appliances. Think of the variety of appliances you can buy today: lamps, electric toasters, electric toothbrushes, electric razors, microwave ovens, dishwashers, food processors, bread machines, stereos, TVs, VCRs, home computers, and on and on and on! In fact, I once saw an advertisement for an electric shoestring tying machine! All of these appliances have different functions, yet they all have one thing in common: a cord with a plug at the end. They are all designed to utilize the same power!

Do they use this power in the same way and to the same extent? No! Each appliance uses its own specific amount of power. Some are 20-watt appliances, some are 1,000-watt appliances. Some use 220 volts, others 110 volts. Some use alternating current, some have transformers built into them that convert house current to 12-volt direct current. The power requirement of each appliance is usually stamped on the back or underside of the appliance. In other words, to paraphrase Ephesians 4:7, appliances are given to us according to the measure of the power available.

The early Christians knew the secret of living by resurrection power, and nothing else will account for the amazing effect they had upon the world of their day. They did not try to borrow power from the world, for they found they had all they could possibly need, available continuously from a risen, triumphant Lord. That is why Paul writes in Ephesians 3:20–21, "Now to him who by the power at work within us is able to do far more abundantly than all that we ask or think . . . be glory in the church."

Paul claims this power for himself as well: "Of this gospel I was made a minister according to the gift of God's grace"—the grace, or spiritual gift given to him—"which was given me by the working of his power" (Ephesians 3:7). The only limit the apostle ever found to this resurrection power was the limit of his faith to receive it. As faith grew his effectiveness grew. He did not always see the results himself, but he trusted God to produce the results, because resurrection power can never fail.

Like no other

Resurrection power is like no other power on earth. It is unique, and has no possible rival. It is a power that operates in the midst of death and despair. It operates when the entire world seems dead and barren. It explodes into life and light in the midst of an empty, dark cemetery—for that is where it was first demonstrated. When Jesus Christ was resurrected, He came out from among the dead. So if you learn to live by resurrection power, you can experience life, hope, and vitality when everything and everyone around you is dead and hopeless.

Resurrection power is a "stealth" power—silent and invisible. It makes no sound, it operates below the radar scope of this world. Other forms of power are noisy and obvious—they pound, pulsate, throb, hum, roar, buzz, or explode. But resurrection power is silent. It accomplishes its purpose without ostentation, flash, pizzazz, or neon lights. Christians who live by resurrection power don't use it to dazzle others or advertise its effects. That's why the distinguishing marks of Christian character are humility and servanthood rather than showiness. Genuine Christians demonstrate the reality of resurrection power through the quiet evidence of their lives: love, joy, peace, endurance under hardships, kindness, goodness, faithfulness, gentleness, and self-control.

God has a marvelous way of illustrating spiritual truth through nature. He demonstrates His resurrection power every year through every returning springtime. Out of the cold, barren, death of winter, God brings new life, color, warmth, and glory by means of a quiet, invisible force which gradually transforms the whole landscape into a fairyland of beauty.

Resurrection power is irresistible. It cannot be turned aside. It takes absolutely no account of any obstacles thrown in its path, except to use them for further opportunities to advance its cause. When Jesus came bursting from the grave, He didn't give the slightest attention to the obstacles human beings had placed in His way. There was a large stone in front of His tomb; He passed right through it. He was wrapped in yard after yard of linen cloth; He left the graveclothes undisturbed behind Him. There were Roman guards in front of His tomb; He ignored them. He took not the slightest notice of the decrees of Caesar or the orders of Pilate or the fulminations of the Jewish priests.

From his imprisonment in Rome, Paul wrote to the Philippians, "I want you to know, brethren, that what has happened to me has really served to advance the gospel, so that it has become known throughout the whole praetorian guard and to all the rest that my imprisonment is for Christ" (1:12–13). Every effort being made to stop the gospel was really advancing it. Because Paul had learned to depend on the power of Christ's resurrection, he was not in the least disturbed by apparent setbacks. He did not rely upon his own cleverness or upon the influence and intervention of others, but solely upon the ability of a risen Lord to bring about His will in spite of deliberate human attempts to nullify it.

Resurrection power needs no props or support. It does not borrow from any other source, though it uses other forms of power as its instrument. It does not even require a cup of coffee to get started in the morning! There is absolutely nothing else like it anywhere in the universe.

Available by faith

Resurrection power is available to every true Christian by faith. What is faith? It could well be defined as "a human response to a divine promise." Faith is a sense of expectation, a quiet trust that another person will do exactly as he said he would do. The Bible tells us that Abraham "grew strong in his faith as he gave glory to God, fully convinced that God was able to do what he had promised" (Romans 4:20–21).

Many people think that faith has something to do with feelings. "I don't *feel* like I have faith," they say. But faith has nothing to do with feelings, and takes no account of moods or physical conditions. Feelings come and go, rise and fall, but faith endures and perseveres, because it does not look to any human source for help. The object of faith is God alone.

The Christian who believes that a risen Jesus Christ now lives within confidently expects Christ to work through him or her, adding His divine "plus" that marks the presence of resurrection power. Christ will not necessarily be "felt" in an emotional way, but He will be present. He will make ordinary words and actions produce extraordinary results. He will take common relationships and transform them into uncommon accomplishments. He will do exactly as He promised: "exceeding abundantly above all that we ask or think" (Ephesians 3:20 KJV)—not according to our time schedule but according to God's.

Surely this is the missing note in today's church activity. The church is still the church, still the body of Christ, but it has been brainwashed by the world to the point that it has forgotten the divine provision for reaching the world. The church will never again affect the world as it did in the first century until individual Christians begin to utilize the gifts God has given them in the power of the resurrected Lord. This should be the most important thing in the world to all of us as Christians—more important than our standard of living, our worldly success, our desire to travel or find romance or be entertained or anything else.

Paul puts the case clearly in Romans 13: "The night is far gone, the day is at hand. Let us then cast off the works of darkness and put on the armor of light; let us conduct ourselves becomingly as in the day, not in reveling and drunkenness, not in debauchery and licentiousness, not in quarreling and jealousy. But put on the Lord Jesus Christ, and make no provision for the flesh, to gratify its desires" (13:12–14).

In the next chapter we shall learn just how pastors and other church leaders fit into this divine provision for the operation of Christ's body, the church. Be prepared for some surprises!

CHAPTER 7

HOW THE
BODY WORKS

In his letter to the Ephesian Christians, the apostle Paul uses two great figures of speech or word pictures to help us understand the true nature and functioning of the church. The apostle likens the church, first, to a human body of flesh and bones, made up of many members articulated and coordinated together. The apostle likens the church, second, to a building which he describes as growing through the centuries to be a habitation for God through the Spirit.

Is the apostle guilty of mixing his metaphors? Absolutely—much as you and I might if we said, "You buttered your bread, now lie in it!" Buildings don't grow as bodies do—yet I believe Paul has deliberately constructed his word pictures to portray for us a vision of the church as something vital, alive, and organic.

When Paul speaks of the church as a body, he makes it clear that no one joins that body except by a new birth, through faith in Jesus Christ. There is no other way into this body. Once a person becomes a part of that body, every member has a contribution to make. As each member works at the task God has given him to do, the whole body functions as intended.

When Paul describes the church as a building, he makes it clear that it is a *living, growing* building. Every Christian is a stone added to that building—a "living stone," as Peter says in his first letter (see 1 Peter 2:5). Each is a vital part of the great temple the Holy Spirit is building as a habitation for God. We can never understand the church until we grasp that picture.

Many people, seeking to discover God today, say that He is dead. The trouble is, they don't know His present address. They don't know where He lives. But He is very much at home in His body, the building made for Him by the Holy Spirit.

If we think of the church as a body, then Ephesians 4 presents us with an anatomy lesson, a view of the physiology and structure of the body—how the various organs function together, how the parts of the body are coordinated to accomplish the purpose of the body. If we think of the church as a building, then Ephesians 4 shows us the blueprints, the architecture, of the building.

Whether we regard the church as a body or a building, there are four ministries, or functions, within it which are so universally needed and so mutually shared that we must consider them independently from the other gifts that Christ gives to His church. Paul underscores these four particular gifts in verses 11 and 12: "His gifts were that some should be apostles, some prophets, some evangelists, some pastors and teachers, for the equipment of the saints, for the work of ministry, for building up the body of Christ."

These four categories—apostles, prophets,

evangelists, and pastor-teachers—are among the gifts that the risen Lord has imparted to human beings (and which we explored in chapter 4, "All God's Children Have Gifts"). They constitute what we shall call "support gifts" (as contrasted with the "service" and "sign" gifts previously considered, as found in 1 Corinthians 12 and Romans 12). These four gifts relate to the whole body of Christ, much as the major body systems relate to the physical body.

There are, within the human body, four major systems upon which the entire body is dependent for proper functioning: the skeletal and muscular framework, the nerve system, the digestive system, and the circulatory systems. There are other systems in the body that are not essential for life itself (such as the reproductive system), but these four are. In a most remarkable way they correspond to the four support ministries within the body of Christ:

1. "Bones and muscles"—*the gift of apostles*

First, there is the basic structural system of bones and muscles. This gives the body its fundamental support and makes possible our mobility and activity. We would all be nothing but rolling, shapeless globs of gelatin if it were not for our bones and muscles! This image clearly corresponds to the apostles and their function in the body of Christ. Their work was foundational, skeletal. They formed the basic structure that made the body of Christ assume the particular form it has.

To revert for a moment to the figure of the church as a building, there is a clear word from the apostle Paul concerning the function of the apostles and prophets. In Ephesians 2:19 and 20 he says, "So then you are no longer strangers and sojourners, but you are fellow citizens with the saints and members of the household of God, built upon the foundation of the apostles and prophets, Christ Jesus Himself being the chief cornerstone."

The foundation of the church is Jesus Christ, as Paul declared to the Corinthians, "For no other foundation can any one lay than that which is laid, which is Jesus Christ" (1 Corinthians 3:11), and the primary work of an apostle was to declare the whole body of truth concerning Jesus Christ. That is the foundation. What the apostles say about Jesus Christ is the foundation of the church, and what they said about Jesus Christ is recorded for us in the New Testament. That book is written by the apostles and prophets, and the church rests squarely upon that foundation.

How does one get into the church? By believing the truth about Jesus Christ (and believing means more than intellectual assent—it is a commitment of the *will* as well). It is only as the church rests upon this foundation of the faith, as taught by the apostles, that there is any certainty or strength. Today many are straying from the foundation, and as a result they have lost any note of authority or assurance. Merely human viewpoints or opinions do not change the foundation. Modern knowledge and the discoveries of science will never alter it. Our ultimate concern is what the apostles taught. That is the greatest revelation of reality we possess, "the truth [as it] is in Jesus" (Ephesians 4:21).

People in the construction business know that a foundation is of the utmost importance. You do not take risks or shortcuts with a foundation. You lay it squarely, securely, and strongly, for the whole building is going to rest on that foundation and will derive its strength from the character of the foundation. The same is true of the church.

The Lord Jesus made very clear that if a person builds on the wrong foundation, he is in trouble. One man may build his house on the sand, and the house may look very beautiful and impressive, but when the storms come, it falls. Another man may build on the rock, and his house will stand in the storm. The foundation makes all the difference.

Jesus Himself is the one who selected the apostles. In the Gospels we have the record of the Lord calling twelve men to be "with him." That was their primary characteristic as apostles, men who had been with Jesus. He sent them out in a specialized ministry. (The word *apostle* means "one sent out.") The Twelve had a special commission and a special authority. As you follow their ministry, you recognize that they possessed an authoritative word. Wherever they went they spoke with authority. They were impressed with this themselves. They came back to Jesus and told Him how they rejoiced to discover that the demons were subject to them. When they spoke the word, they had authority and that word of authority is the special mark of an apostle.

Paul, of course, was a special apostle, chosen by Jesus after His resurrection. He did not obtain his ministry from the Twelve but directly from the Lord Himself, though what he taught and preached was in no sense different from what the Twelve proclaimed.

The apostolic gift is still being given today, though in a secondary sense. There is no new truth to be added to the Scriptures. But the body of truth which we now have is to be taken by those who have an apostolic gift and imparted to new churches wherever they may begin. It is part of the apostolic gift to start new churches. We call those who perform this ministry "church planters" and "pioneer missionaries" today. Throughout the course of church history, there have been many such secondary apostles, including Adoniram Judson in Burma, William Carey in India, and Hudson Taylor in China. These were Christians with the apostolic gift, and they were made responsible for imparting the whole faith to new churches.

To return to the figure of the body, this apostolic system of truth is the bones and muscles of the church. There is no other line of truth about Jesus Christ. There is no other information that can come to us about Jesus than what the apostles have given. Any other claim, as Paul says to the Galatians, "is another gospel" (see Acts 4:12; Galatians 1:7). Here is the skeleton of the body, and upon this the church is built, and from this comes its strength.

2. "The nervous system"—*the gift of prophets*

Linked with the skeletal system in the human body is the nervous system. It is the means by which the bones and muscles are stimulated to activity. The nervous system is the directive system. It is linked directly to the head, and from there it conveys messages to every part of the body. This system corresponds to the work of prophets in the body of Christ.

A prophet is essentially a person who speaks for God, who unfolds the mind of God. In the early church, before the New Testament was written down, prophets spoke directly by the inspiration of the Holy Spirit, uttering the truths that are now recorded in the New Testament. They unfolded what God taught, and thus the body was motivated, galvanized into action.

Such men as Mark, Luke, James, and Jude were not themselves prophets, they were associated with the apostles in the writing of the New Testament.

The gift of a prophet differs from that of an apostle: The apostle gives an authoritative declaration of the whole body of truth concerning Jesus Christ; but the prophet interprets that authoritative word and explains the truth so that it becomes very clear and compelling. The very word *prophet* suggests this. It derives from a Greek root that means "to cause to shine," and is linked with the prefix "pro-" which means "before." Thus a prophet is one who stands before and causes the word of the apostle to shine.

This meaning of the word *prophet* is fully reflected in Peter's second letter when he says, "We have the prophetic word made more sure. You will do well to pay attention to this as to a lamp shining in a dark place" (2 Peter 1:19). Paul clarifies it further, "He who prophesies speaks to men for their upbuilding and encouragement and consolation" (1 Corinthians 14:3).

The church owes much to the ministry of prophets. Not only were parts of the Scriptures given to us by prophets but the great theologians and preachers of the church have been people with prophetic gifts. Men such as Martin Luther, John Calvin, John Wesley, and the founders of other denominations have been prophets, and many pastors and Bible teachers today have prophetic gifts. Usually men who speak at conferences are speaking as prophets, making the truth clear, shining, and gripping. They differ from teachers in that the prophet tends more to deal with the great sweeping principles of Scripture and reality, leaving the development of more specific areas to the teacher.

3. "The digestive system"—*the gift of evangelists*

The third support ministry within the body of Christ is the evangelist. He is linked with the work of the pastor-teacher. Evangelists and teaching pastors work together just as the apostles and prophets work together. Evangelists are men and women with a special gift of communicating the gospel in relevant terms to those who are not yet Christians. Since the evangelist is primarily responsible for the numerical growth of the body of Christ, the ministry of the evangelist corresponds to the digestive system within the human body, taking food that is quite unlike flesh and transforming it into flesh and bones, making it a living part of the body.

All Christians are expected to evangelize, but not all have the gift of an evangelist. Christians are to evangelize as witnesses, but a witness is different from an evangelist. Any individual Christian should be able to explain to others what happened when he or she became a Christian. As the apostle Peter says, a Christian should "be ready always to give . . . a reason of the hope that is in you" (1 Peter 3:15 KJV). Witnessing should be as easy as talking about any other meaningful life experience. If you can talk about how wonderful your husband is, or your wife is, or your children or grandchildren are, you can witness for Christ. To talk about your Christian experience simply and naturally is Christian witnessing.

But the gift of an evangelist goes further. He knows how to explain the why and how of the great redeeming story of Jesus Christ. He is able to proclaim the truth that results in new birth. He is forever dealing with the truth that God has not left humanity in a hopeless condition but has made a way—at great and incredible cost to His Son!—by which men and women can be set free from sin and death, and given a new start and a new basis for the battle. That is the work of an evangelist.

The evangelist's task is not to go about denouncing sin, but to point the way out of sin. The evangelist may call people's attention to that which is creating so much misery and heartache in their lives, but his work is not to condemn sinners. Evangelists are not to thunder away at people, telling them what miserable creatures they are and how God is waiting to strike them with thunderbolts of judgment. He is not to expose the horrors of hellfire and dangle sinners over those fires until they writhe and tremble. That is not the calling of the evangelist!

If the preaching of "fire and brimstone" is ever called for, it is the task of a prophet, not the task of an evangelist. The evangelist's role is to tell people about the overpowering grace of God and the overpowering love of the heavenly Father—a Father who calls men and women back to Himself, offering to set their twisted lives straight through the redeeming work of Jesus Christ.

Many Christians today possess the gift of an evangelist, both men and women. Evangelism can be done anywhere. It is not restricted to mass meetings, such as in the great Billy Graham crusades, though Dr. Graham's ministry is also true evangelism. The gift of an evangelist can be exercised toward a single individual, as is clear in the book of Acts when Philip the evangelist spoke to the Ethiopian eunuch and told him of the saving grace of Jesus Christ.

4. "The circulatory system"—*the gift of pastor-teachers*

The fourth great physical system which the body depends upon for life is the circulatory system—the veins and arteries linked to the heart and lungs, which distribute food and oxygen to every part of the body, and take away the accumulated wastes. This corresponds to the work of teaching pastors within the body of Christ, who are there to maintain the life of the body by feeding and cleansing it and preserving its life in vigor and vitality.

The word *pastor* means "shepherd." The pastor is also called in the Scriptures an elder, as well as an overseer or bishop. These last two are the same Greek word, translated in two different ways. "Bishop" is the English translation of *episcopus*, which literally means "overseer." Elders or bishops were always limited to one locality, one church, in New Testament days. A man who was an elder or pastor in one church was not also an elder in another place.

Nor were these always men who devoted their full time to ministry. Some elders were called ruling elders and were often supported by the church to devote full time to their work, though this was not always the case. There were also others who were elders but were not called ruling elders. These included anyone who did shepherding work within the church. Today, we would see these shepherding elders as Sunday school teachers, home Bible class leaders, and young people's leaders. Many Christians have the gift of pastor-teacher whether they are employed full-time in that capacity or not.

The ruling elders correspond most closely to the present concept of a pastor, but in the early church there was never a single pastor or elder but always several. They were to serve as teachers and administrators—but they were *not* to be, as Peter says, "domineering over those in your charge" (1 Peter 5:3). In other words, they are not to be church bosses. They are not to act as the final authority within the church so that whatever they say goes. Jesus Himself taught this. Mark records that Jesus called the disciples to Him and said, "You know that those who are supposed to rule over the Gentiles lord it over them, and their great men exercise authority over them. But it shall not be so among you" (Mark 10:42–43).

The pastors of the churches are not to exercise their authority as bosses but as *examples.* When they themselves obey the Word, others will be motivated to follow. But if the teaching pastors do not practice what they preach, they have no other authority. Their authority derives from their spirituality, and if they lose their spirituality they also lose their authority. It is not the office that gives a pastor the right to rule—it is the individual and his gift before God. This question of a pastor's authority is so important and so misunderstood among the churches that I want to take the time here to comment further on how the Scriptures view the matter.

No command structure

Authority among Christians is not derived from the same source as worldly authority, nor is it to be exercised in the same manner. The world's view of authority places men over one another, as in a military command structure, a business executive hierarchy, or a governmental system. This is as it should be. Urged by the competitiveness created by the fall of the human race, and faced with the rebelliousness and ruthlessness of sinful human nature, the world could not function without the use of command structures and executive decisionmaking.

But as Jesus carefully and clearly stated, "It shall not be so among you." Disciples are always in a different relationship to one another than are the "worldlings," those who are outside of the church. Christians are brothers and sisters, children of one Father and members of one another in the body of Christ. Jesus put it clearly in Matthew 23:8, "You have one teacher, and you are all brethren."

Throughout twenty centuries the church has virtually ignored these words. Probably with the best of intentions, it has repeatedly borrowed the authority structures of the world, changed the names of executives from kings, generals, captains, presidents, governors, secretaries, heads and chiefs to popes, patriarchs, bishops, stewards, deacons, pastors, and elders, and gone merrily on its way, lording it over the laity and destroying the model of servanthood that our Lord intended.

In most churches today, an unthinking acceptance has been given to the idea that the pastor is the final voice of authority in both doctrine and practice, and that he is the executive officer of the church with respect to administration. But surely, if a pope over the whole church is bad, a pope in every church is no better!

But if the church is not to imitate the world in this matter, what is it to do? Leadership must certainly be exercised within the church, and there must be some form of authority. The question is answered in Jesus' words, "You have one teacher." For much too long churches have behaved as if Jesus were far away in heaven having left it up to church leaders to make their own decisions and run their own affairs.

But Jesus left the church with a far different vision of church leadership when He assured the disciples in the Great Commission, "Lo, I am with you always, to the close of the age." And in Matthew 18:20, He reiterated, "Where two or three are gathered in my name, there am I in the midst of them." Clearly this indicates that He is present not only in the church as a whole but in every local church as well. It is Jesus Himself, therefore, who is the ultimate authority within every body of Christians. He is quite prepared to exercise His authority through the instrument He Himself has ordained: the eldership.

The task of the elders is *not* to run the church themselves but to determine how the Lord in their midst wishes to run His church! Much of this He has already made known through the Scriptures that describe the impartation and exercise of spiritual gifts and the availability of resurrection power to exercise those gifts. He has also made known through the Scriptures the responsibility of believers to bear one another's burdens, to confess their sins to one another, to teach, to admonish, and to encourage one another, to hold one another accountable, and to evangelize and serve the needs of a hurting world.

The mind of the Spirit

In the day-to-day decisions that face every church, elders are to seek and find the mind of the Lord through an uncoerced unanimity, reached after thorough and biblically-related discussion. Thus, ultimate authority—even in the practical, day-to-day operation of the church—is vested in the Lord and in no one else. This is what the book of Acts reveals in its description of the actions of the Holy Spirit who planned, initiated, and ordered the amazingly effective evangelism strategy of the early church (see especially Acts chapters 8 and 13).

The elders of the early church sought the mind of the Spirit and, when the Spirit made His will clear to them, they acted with unity of thought and purpose, as we see in Acts 15:28: "For it has seemed good to the Holy Spirit and to us to lay upon you no greater burden." The authority, therefore, was not the authority of men but of God, expressed not through men, acting as individuals, but through the collective agreement of men whom the Spirit had led to eldership (see Acts 20:28).

The point is simply this: No one person is the sole expression of the mind of the Spirit; no individual has authority from God to direct the affairs of the church. Whenever a church gathers itself around the unquestioned leadership of a single individual, it ceases to be a church; it becomes a cult. A plurality of elders is necessary as a safeguard to the all-too-human tendency to play God and lord one's authority over other people.

Even when a plurality of elders is established, care must be taken that the church's leaders (who, biblically, are to be seen as servants, not bosses) exercise their authority with humility, not by dominating, controlling, and intimidating others. The influence of a servant-leader is not the power to give orders but the ability to inspire enthusiasm and voluntary cooperation. This is the nature of *all* authority among Christians—even the authority of the Lord Himself! He never forces our obedience, He attracts our devotion and our love—and

He does so by awakening in us our gratitude and our responsiveness to *His* love. "We love, because he first loved us" (1 John 4:19).

The true authority of elders and other leaders in the church is that of respect, aroused by their own loving and godly example. This is the force of two verses often cited by those who claim a unique authority of pastors over church members. The first is found in 1 Thessalonians 5:12–13: "But we beseech you, brethren, to respect those who labor among you and are over you in the Lord and admonish you, and to esteem them very highly in love because of their work."

The key phrase is "and are over you in the Lord," and the Greek word in question is *prohistamenous.* Though this is translated "over you" in both the Revised Standard Version and King James Version, the word itself contains no implication of being over another. The New English Bible more properly renders it, "and in the Lord's fellowship are your leaders and counsellors." The thought in the word is that of "standing before" others, not of "ruling over" them. It is the common word for leadership. In the body of Christ, leaders can lead only if they are able to persuade some to follow.

Another verse used to support command authority is Hebrews 13:17, which the Revised Standard Version renders, "Obey your leaders and submit to them; for they are keeping watch over your souls, as men who will have to give account." The imperative translated "obey" is from the word *peitho,* to persuade. In the middle voice, as used here, Thayer's lexicon gives its meaning as "to suffer one's self to be persuaded." Again there is no thought of a right to command someone against his will. But the clear thrust is that leaders are persuaders whose ability to persuade arises not from a smooth tongue or a dominant personality but from a personal walk that evokes respect.

Why change now?

At this point many may be tempted to say, "What difference does it make? After all, the pattern of command authority is too widely established to alter now. Besides, many churches seem to be doing all right as it is. Why try to change now?"

In response, consider the following:

1. The Bible indicates that any deviation from the divine plan inevitably produces weakness, division, strife, increasing fruitlessness, and, ultimately, death. The present low state of many churches is testimony to the effects of ignoring, over a long period of time, God's pattern for the church.

2. A command structure of authority in the church deprives the world of any model or demonstration of a different way of life than the one it already lives by. Unbelievers see no difference between the church and the world, so why should they change and believe in Jesus Christ?

3. A command authority inevitably produces resentment, repression, exploitation and, finally, rebellion. Command authority is an expression of law, not grace. The Scriptures assure us that law can never redeem or restore us; by its very nature, the law can only condemn and repress us.

4. The Lord Jesus desires to use the church to show the world a wholly new form of authority that is consistent with grace, not law. But this new form of authority is nullified by the top-down, command-style

structure that prevails in today's church. Our dying-to-live gospel is pronounced D.O.A.—dead on arrival—even before it is proclaimed, because we deny its power with the way we conduct our lives and our church business. As a result, God is robbed of His glory and His image is distorted before the watching world. Nothing could be more serious than this!

Note that each of the four support ministries we are discussing have to do with the Word of God. The first two—apostles and prophets—are concerned with originating and expounding the Word, while the last two—evangelists and pastor-teachers—are concerned with applying the Word to individual lives. The evangelist deals with the beginning of Christian life while the teaching pastor is involved with the development and growth of that life. Evangelists are much like obstetricians, helping to bring new Christians into the world. Teaching pastors are like pediatricians, seeing that these Christians have a healthy spiritual "diet," that their "diseases" receive proper attention, and that they get plenty of spiritual "fresh air" and "exercise."

To return to the word picture of the church as a building, the evangelist is the quarryman who digs out the rock, cuts it loose from quarrystone, and hews it to a rough approximation of its final size. The pastor-teacher is the stone mason who shapes the rock, fitting it into the building in its proper place according to the blueprint of the great architect.

When we compare present-day churches to the original blueprint, it is strikingly apparent that many deviations have been permitted that have been detrimental to the life of the church. Through the centuries, the church gradually turned from the simple provisions that made it such a powerful and compelling force in its early years, and terrible distortions entered into the church that continue to weaken the church today. Popular thinking fastened onto the church *building*—the physical stone-and-glass edifice—as the identifying symbol of the church. Emphasis was placed upon great imposing structures, massive ornate cathedrals with stained glass windows and flying buttresses.

In the beginning, "working in the church" meant to exercise a gift or perform a ministry anywhere within the far-flung body of Christ—even in a home, out on a mission field, or in a hospital. Gradually, however, "working in the church" came to mean performing some religious act within a specific building called "the church."

At the same time, there was a gradual transfer of ministry responsibility from the people (whom we now call the *laity*) to the few pastor-teachers (whom we now call the *clergy*, a term derived from the Latin *clericus*, meaning "priest"). The scriptural concept that *every* believer is a priest before God was gradually lost, and a special class of super-Christians emerged who were looked to for practically everything, and who came to be called the "ministry." Somehow, the church lost sight of the concept, so clearly stated in Ephesians 4, that *all* Christians are "in the ministry." The proper task of the four support ministries we have examined is to train, motivate, and strengthen the people—so-called "ordinary laypeople"—to do the work of the ministry.

When the ministry was left to the "professionals," there was nothing left for the people to do other than come to church and listen. They were told that it was their responsibility to bring the world into the church building to hear the pastor preach the gospel. Soon Christianity became little more than a Sunday-morning spectator sport, much like the definition of football: twenty-two men down on the field, desperately in need of rest, and twenty thousand in the grandstands, desperately in need of exercise.

This unbiblical distortion has placed pastors under an unbearable burden. They have proved completely unequal to the task of evangelizing the world, counseling the wounded and brokenhearted, ministering to the poor and needy, relieving the oppressed and afflicted, expounding the Scriptures, and challenging the entrenched forces of evil in an increasingly darkened world. Pastors were never, ever meant to do it all! To even attempt it is to end up frustrated, exhausted, and emotionally drained—which, of course, is exactly the state in which you find many pastors today!

Further, this distortion has resulted in a sadly impoverished church that has made little impact on the world and increasingly withdraws into weakness, irrelevance, and isolation. We desperately need to return to the dynamic of the early church. We can no longer defend our ivy-clad traditions which leave no room for the original, power-packed New Testament strategy. Pastors, particularly, must restore to the people the ministry that was taken from them with the best of intentions.

The work of the ministry belongs to the *entire* body of believers, who should be equipped, guided, and encouraged by those who are gifted by God to expound and apply His Word with wisdom and power. The entire body has received gifts from the Spirit, and it is the task of those in the pastoral ministry to encourage the entire body to discover and exercise those gifts. When we rediscover the pattern and strategy of Ephesians 4, when we have given all Christians in the body their God-given role as ministers of God's eternal plan, then the entire body comes alive with resurrection power. Lives are changed. Ministries explode. Communities are touched and healed. The church becomes healthy and vital and exciting again.

If we can recapture God's original strategy for the church, then we will again see churches that are modern extensions of the church of Acts. The trademarks of the true, living church of Jesus Christ are boldness, power, transformation, and love, lived out in act after act of Christian service. There is no place in this world more exciting to be than a church that operates as God designed it to!

In the next chapter, we will see how all the members of the body of Christ can be "shaped up" to do the ministry of the church.

CHAPTER 8

SHAPING UP THE SAINTS

Throughout the Christian centuries, no principle of church life has proved more revolutionary—and more bitterly fought!—than the declaration of Ephesians 4 that the ultimate work of the church in the world is to be done by the saints—plain, ordinary Christians—and not by a professional clergy or a few select laypeople. We must never lose the impact of the apostle Paul's statement that apostles, prophets, evangelists, and pastor-teachers exist "for the equipment of the saints for the work of ministry, for building up the body of Christ (Ephesians 4:12).

Perhaps this can be made clearer if we diagram verses 11 and 12 in the following manner:

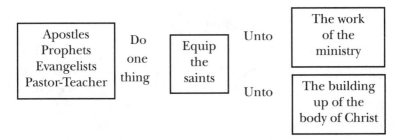

Note that neither the apostles and prophets nor the evangelists and pastor-teachers are expected to do the work of the ministry! They are not even expected to do the work of building up the body of Christ! Those tasks are to be done only by the people—the ordinary, plain-vanilla Christians we often call "the laity." The four offices of apostle, prophet, evangelist, and pastor-teacher exist for one function and one function only: to equip everyday Christians to do the work God has given them—and *gifted* them!—to do.

So let's take a closer look at the word *equipping*. What does this mean and how is it done? In the original Greek, the word is *katartismon*, from which we get our English word *artisan*—an artist or craftsman, someone who works with his hands to make or build things. It is a special point of interest that this word first appears in the New Testament in connection with the calling of the disciples.

As Jesus walked along the Sea of Galilee, He saw two pairs of brothers, Peter and Andrew, and James and John, sitting in a boat busily working. What were they doing? They were mending their nets. The word *mending* is the word translated in Ephesians 4 as "equipping." They were equipping their nets by mending them. They were fixing their nets, making them strong, preparing them for service, getting them ready for action!

Mending the saints

The use of this particular word suggests that the role of the four support gifts within the church is essentially that of *mending the saints*, preparing them for service, getting them ready for action. This Greek word is also translated as "fitting them out" or "preparing." The Greek authority, J. H. Thayer, says it means "to make one what he ought to be." Perhaps the nearest modern equivalent is "to shape up." The ultimate aim of apostles, prophets, evangelists, and pastor-teachers is the shaping up of the saints to do the work of the ministry.

A moment's thought will make clear that the instrument to be used by the four support gifts in equipping the saints is the Word of God. Obviously, all four support ministries relate somehow to that Word. The apostles and prophets originated and expounded it. As we have noted, they laid the foundations upon which the whole church must rest. The ministry of the apostles is still available to us through the written New Testament, and prophets are still given by the Holy Spirit to the churches to unfold the word of the apostles and make it clear and powerful.

Evangelists and pastor-teachers are to proclaim and apply the Word. Evangelists move about, some more widely than others, telling the great historic story of what God has done for men and women in Jesus Christ, and describing what will result in the life of anyone who believes this story. Evangelists also have a responsibility to take with them younger Christians who share the gift of an evangelist, and to mentor them and train them in how to proclaim the good news effectively in the power of a risen Lord.

The task of the pastor-teacher is to use the Word of God to cleanse and feed the flock. The early church clearly understood that the Word of God was the instrument of growth in the lives of Christians. Paul once spoke to the very elders to whom this Ephesian letter is addressed and said to them, "I commend you to God and to the word of his grace, which is able to build you up and to give you the inheritance among all those who are sanctified" (Acts 20:32).

And again, at the close of his career, he wrote to his son in the faith, young Timothy, and urged him to teach the inspired Scriptures which were given, that the man of God may be complete, equipped for every good work. If pastors and teachers ignore the Word, God's divinely-provided instrument of equipping, then they should not be surprised if the saints in their charge are ill-equipped for—and ineffective in—the work of the ministry. That is why so many churches today are little more than spectator arenas where unequipped, unmotivated, uninvolved people sit around, waiting only to be kept amused and occupied.

The whole truth

The teaching of the truth of the Word of God is what Peter calls "feeding the flock of God which is among you" (1 Peter 5:2 KJV). The Word can both feed (Hebrews 5:12–13 and 1 Peter 2:2) and cleanse (John 15:3 and Ephesians 5:26), and the true pastor will constantly be using it to do both. He will seek to teach the whole truth of God. There is no better means to do this than through the expository preaching of the whole Bible. The expository method of teaching or preaching is to go through a book, or a section of a book of the Bible, leaving out nothing, commenting on everything, touching it all. That prevents a pastor from skewing his preaching only to a few favorite "pet passages," and it forces that pastor to keep truth in balance.

The prophet Isaiah says that this was the way Scripture was originally given: "Precept upon precept, precept upon precept, line upon line, line upon line, here a little, there a little" (Isaiah 28:13). You won't find in the Bible a chapter on evil and another on morals and another on baptism and another on marriage. These subjects are all woven together in delightful harmony. One can never take a sizable section of the Word of God and comment on it without presenting truth in balance. It is *truth in balance* that performs the task of equipping the saints.

The business of preaching is, as someone has well put it, "to comfort the afflicted and afflict the comfortable." The truth is very comforting and enlightening, but it also ought to get under our collars, and into our hearts, and disturb us greatly at times. Only the Word of God can do this.

It is the pounding of the hammer of the Word that finally pulverizes the granite hardness of our rationalizing, self-deceptive hearts, making us yield to what God is saying to us. It is the truth, driven home by a heart made earnest in prayer, that melts, softens, and heals hearts, causing individuals to grow in grace and power. Only the Word of God can teach a new Christian the difference between flashy, dedicated zeal operating in the suave power of the flesh, and the quiet commitment of a Spirit-filled life that faithfully obeys God whether anyone sees and applauds or not.

Unfortunately, in many churches (and particularly American churches), there has come a strange reversal of roles between the pastor and the evangelist. The work of evangelism has been exalted over that of pastoral teaching in many American churches. This has effectively deprived churches of the biblical ministry of a pastor and has resulted in a sadly impoverished, untaught, unequipped people. How did this come about?

In frontier America, the role of evangelist was greatly admired and respected. So pastors of frontier churches began to see their role as that of an evangelist, whose task was to declare the initial truths of Christianity and win as many to Christ as possible. They began to evangelize in their pulpits, priding themselves on their faithfulness to their calling in proclaiming the gospel fearlessly, Sunday after Sunday. As a result, it became the task of the people to bring others into the church to hear the pastor evangelize. In time, however, fewer and fewer unchurched people came into the church. Finally, the pastor was left to evangelize the evangelized—week after week after week!

Since the saints were not led on into a deeper and clearer understanding of the great provisions of life and power available to them through the Spirit, they grew dull and bored with the gospel they heard every week. They soon fell into apathy, criticism, quarreling, bickering, divisions, and schisms, and eventually into dissolute living and the double standards of hypocrisy.

When this occurred, the rate of conversions dropped off alarmingly, and an evangelist was usually brought in to correct this. The visiting evangelist, however, frequently found that the people were in no spiritual condition to undertake evangelism, and so he had to take a week or so of special meetings with the congregation and become a pastor to them, teaching them enough about the spiritual life that they could aid him in the subsequent outreach meetings. Thus the modern revivalist was born. The annual "revival" became the shot in the arm upon which most churches depended for any degree of advance or witness.

Naturally this picture is somewhat overdrawn, and the situation just described was not true everywhere, nor always to the same degree. There have always been strong churches where the pastor has faithfully taught and applied the Scriptures, and where Christians have demonstrated a quality of life that has made their community sit up and take notice.

Obviously, I would never wish to downgrade the splendid work of evangelism that has gone on for many decades in certain great preaching centers. Under their ministry thousands have found spiritual rebirth and have gone further and deeper into the truths of Scripture, becoming effective, ministering Christians. Unfortunately, however, the good is all too often the enemy of the best. When the pastor becomes an evangelist and the evangelist is forced to assume the role of pastor, neither is performing his proper function within the body. Neither is using his gifts as God planned, and the whole body suffers as a result.

There are, of course, individuals who have both the gifts of an evangelist and a pastor. These people are responsible to use *both* gifts in their ministries. But they should clearly understand that one gift is exercised toward Christians while the other is directed to reaching non-Christians. One is best performed in a meeting of Christians, while the other is best taken outside the church, to the marketplaces and neighborhoods where the worldlings gather.

In all the years I pastored Peninsula Bible Church, we never held an evangelistic meeting in the church. You might think, "Well, it must have been a static church. Without evangelistic meetings, there couldn't have been many new converts at PBC!" But in that, you would be very mistaken! Even without evangelistic meetings, PBC experienced a steady stream of new converts coming into the church for instruction and development in the Christian life. Where, then, did evangelism take place at PBC? Evangelism occurred in the homes of members, in public halls, over the backyard fence, on the school campuses, and wherever a hearing for the gospel could be obtained.

Every meeting held in the church building at PBC has been aimed at the instruction, training, or worship of Christians together. Our entire Sunday school is set up to equip the saints, of all ages, to do the work of the ministry. The work of expounding and applying the Scriptures begins with the pulpit and is continued in every class, in every gathering, and in many of the homes of Christians. Stress is laid upon confronting life as it is really lived in the trenches, so that the insights of Scripture can be applied to real situations, and so that believers can discover how to draw upon the resurrection power of an ever-present Lord. Christians are taught to welcome contact with the world but to live distinctive lives in the midst of it, "sheep in the midst of wolves," as Jesus put it.

Certainly the primary responsibility for effective Christian training lies with those within the church who have the gift of pastor-teacher. Ideally this would include all the ruling elders, plus Sunday school teachers, young people's leaders, home Bible class teachers, small group leaders, and the like. They share together the responsibility of growing in the knowledge of the Word of God and of learning to impart it so as to instruct, admonish, rebuke, exhort, and encourage those who are under their care.

Little tin gods

The Scriptures also tell us the kind of heart and attitude which pastors are to have as they work to "shape up the saints" for ministry. If that phrase, "shaping up the saints," conveys to you an image of a church drill sergeant, thundering, growling, and barking at his people, then you have the wrong idea! Pastors are not to be tyrants or bosses—even though, as we survey the ecclesiastical landscape, we can see more than a few such pastors around!

There was just such a first-century "church boss" mentioned in the apostle John's third letter. His name was Diotrephes, and he was described as a man "who loves to have the preeminence" in the church (3 John 9). In today's church, "bosses" like Diotrephes can be found among both pastors and laypeople—and both are equally destructive to the life, spirit, and vitality of a church.

The apostle Peter writes to certain pastors (or elders) as being himself "a fellow elder with you," and he exhorts them: "I urge you then to see that your 'flock of God' is properly fed and cared for. Accept the responsibility of looking after them willingly and not because you feel you can't get out of it, doing your work not for what you can make, but because you are really concerned for their well being. You should aim not at being 'little tin gods' but as examples of Christian living in the eyes of the flock committed to your charge" (1 Peter 5:2–3 PHILLIPS).

"Little tin gods" is a colorful modern expression for the Greek, "not as lords over God's heritage." The RSV renders it "not as domineering over those in your charge."

You can see that the Peter speaking here is quite different from the brash disciple of the Gospels. Here, chastened and humbled, he seeks to fulfill the commission the Lord Jesus gave him after the resurrection when He asked Peter three times, "Do you love me?" and three times gave him the command, "Feed my sheep." Peter has now learned that the task of the shepherd is to *feed* the sheep—*not to fleece them!* He has learned to be a servant and not a lord over God's people.

These words are not to be taken lightly. Every pastor, especially, must heed these words. Church leaders must ever remember that they are not called to be bosses. They are but instruments, servants, and examples. Once again, Jesus said, "When the good shepherd puts forth his sheep, he goes before them" (see John 10:4). That is, he leads his sheep by doing everything first. No teacher has the right to teach whose life does not exemplify his teaching. If he tries to say one thing and be another, the Chief Shepherd will suddenly pull the rug from under him and his ministry will be despised.

Again, the ministry of shepherding and teaching must be done without desiring personal glory. How well pastors know that right here is where the full force of temptation to pride can strike! There is something very pleasing to the ego to stand in front of others and have every eye fastened on you and every ear open to what you have to say. It is terribly easy to begin to crave that feeling and to find subtle ways of nurturing and encouraging it.

As a pastor I must confess that I had to stop the practice of going to the door after a service and greeting people as they went out. I found that when I did it regularly, it fed my ego in such a way that I had a terrible battle with pride. People were saying nice things to me, and I found myself loving to hear them. It is very easy for a pastor or teacher to perform his ministry for hidden reasons of personal prestige or glory.

Pastors love to be regarded as dedicated, mature Christians. They easily succumb to such thinking as, "I've sacrificed so much time and money to fulfill my calling. Maybe I really do deserve all this attention and praise! After all, haven't I been faithful to God's call on my life? Haven't I done a good job of serving these people and God? Hey, I must be a pretty good guy!"

Of course, no pastor would ever say so publicly. But it is often evident in the hurt feelings they display when something doesn't go their way, or in their desire to quit if they haven't been sufficiently appreciated and applauded. You can see it in the little jabs of jealous cattiness and pettiness which one pastor will sometimes display toward another pastor's ministry. You can sense it in the sarcasm you'll often hear in a pastor's personal speech, and in the false modesty that is often displayed in the pulpit.

I once heard of a congregation that gave its pastor a medal for humility—but they took it away because he wore it! Humility is a tricky commodity: The moment you realize you have it, it's gone!

To get attention

One further thing can be said about the ministry of equipping the saints through the exposition of the Word of God. Paul describes his own ministry in these terms: "Him [Christ] we proclaim, warning every man and teaching every man in all wisdom, that we may present every man mature in Christ" (Colossians 1:28). The process Paul followed in shaping up the saints was first to warn them and then to teach them. Teaching alone—the imparting of biblically correct doctrine—is not enough. It must be preceded by the ministry of *warning*.

You might say, "Warning? Before teaching? That doesn't seem right!" Well, it didn't seem right to me either, the first time I deeply considered this verse in Colossians. Surely, we should teach first, and then, if the teaching is not received, it is appropriate to warn of the results of neglecting that teaching. But when I looked more closely at the meaning of the original word translated "warning," I found that it is the Greek word for "mind" combined with the verb "to put." It means "to put in mind" or to call attention to something. It indicates that the first task of a teacher or pastor is to *capture the attention and sustain the interest of his hearers.*

There is a well-worn story about a grizzled old mule-skinner who wanted to train his mule. The first thing he did was pick up a big board and give the mule a resounding wallop between the ears. As the mule staggered to its knees, a horrified bystander ran up and said, "That's no way to treat an animal! Why did you do that?"

"If you're gonna teach a mule," said the mule-skinner, "you first gotta get his undivided attention."

That's exactly what the apostle suggests our first task is in teaching the Word: get the listener's undivided attention, awaken his or her interest, excite his or her enthusiasm. But I hasten to add: Don't use a board! The people in your church are not mules!

When Paul went to Athens to preach to the sophisticated Greeks (see Acts 17), he didn't begin by climbing Mars Hill and declaring, "Ladies and gentlemen of Athens, I have come to speak to you about the moral superiority of Christianity to paganism!" Yes, that was the subject of his address—but he didn't begin that way! It would have turned off his hearers.

Instead, Paul thought carefully about how to reach his hearers. He put himself in their shoes, and tried to see life from their perspective. He first walked through the city, soaking up perceptions and gaining an understanding of Athenian culture and values. Then, when he got up to speak to the people of Athens, he began by affirming them. "You people of Athens are certainly very religious," he said. "As I have walked around this city, I have seen altars everywhere. I even found one erected to an Unknown God, which clearly indicates there is something about God that you don't yet know, and that is what I have come to talk to you about" (Acts 17:22–23, author's paraphrase.)

Now Paul had their attention! He "put them in mind" of what he wanted to announce. He demonstrated that the key to effective teaching and communication is to first awaken interest and arouse attention.

One of the most amazing illustrations of the power of the ministry of equipping the saints is recorded in Acts 19. There Luke describes the ministry of Paul in the city of Ephesus—the very city to which Paul writes his letter describing the functioning of the church and the ministry of the saints. In Ephesus, says Acts 19:8–10, Paul "entered the synagogue and for three months spoke boldly, arguing and pleading about the kingdom of God; but when some were stubborn and disbelieved, speaking evil of the Way [that is, the Christian faith] before the congregation, he withdrew from them, taking the disciples with him, and argued daily in the hall of Tyrannus. This continued for two years."

Some ancient manuscripts of this passage in Acts read a little differently: "taking the disciples with him, he argued daily in the hall of Tyrannus, from the fifth hour to the tenth." That would mean that Paul taught these new Christians for five hours a day, every day, for two years. That adds up to some 3,650 hours of teaching. Is it any wonder that the tenth verse concludes, "so that all the residents of Asia heard the word of the Lord, both Jews and Greeks."

In other words, during Paul's two years in Ephesus, everyone who lived in the Roman province of Asia (of which Ephesus was the capital) heard the gospel! They didn't all believe, of course, but they all heard. Did Paul reach all of those thousands of people by himself? Of course not! He remained in Ephesus, teaching five hours a day. But the people he taught, the multitudes of common ordinary "saints" who learned from Paul day by day, then fanned out from Ephesus in the normal pursuit of their business. These tradespeople, merchants, farmers, and city officials who were evangelized and discipled by Paul went out along the highways and into the countryside of Asia, not as missionaries but as ordinary laypeople. They exercised their spiritual gifts with such quiet but irresistible power—resurrection power—that the whole province was stirred by the amazing news of the gospel! Many responded, were baptized, and then placed themselves under the teaching of the apostle Paul.

That is how the gospel spread. That is how the first-century world was turned upside down by the early church. That is how the church grew—not by simple addition, but by multiplication, by compounding, by orders of magnitude.

That is the kind of transforming power the church can wield once again—if we are willing to return to the biblical pattern, and to return the ministry of the church to the saints.

CHAPTER 9

THE WORK
OF THE MINISTRY

Many are asking today, "Where is Jesus Christ at work in our world? How does He touch the problems of society today, at the end of the twentieth century?"

The answer is that He is at work *exactly* as He was at work in His lifetime on earth, carrying out precisely the same strategy! Two thousand years ago, He did His work through one solitary, earthly, physical body. Today, He carries on the same work through a complex, many-faceted, corporate body that exists around the world, permeating and penetrating every level of society. It is called "the church," the body of Christ—but its ministry is to the same human race that Jesus ministered to, experiencing the same issues and conditions, facing the same attitudes and problems.

As we have already seen, our Lord has endowed His corporate body with an array of spiritual gifts, capable of many combinations, and designed to establish and improve relationships between any individual and God. Our Lord has also provided the members of His body with a new kind of power—resurrection power!—that operates silently yet powerfully as a result of Christ's life within every believer. It is only when a Christian uses His spiritual gifts in resurrection power that His life becomes an extension of the incarnate life of Jesus. At all other times, His activity is only that of the "natural" man without spiritual effect or power.

Reaching the world

To focus on the gifts of the Spirit and the power in which they operate, we must not lose sight of the twofold reason for the manifestation of these gifts. These are clearly stated as: (1) unto the work of the ministry, and (2) unto the building up of the body of Christ. The gifts are given to be useful in these two realms, the world and the church. We must continually remember that the work of the ministry is to the world. The church exists as God's instrument to reach the world. "For God so loved the world that he gave his only Son" (John 3:16).

It is clearly God's intention that, through the true church, the world might see Jesus Christ at work. The world needs His ministry desperately, but He never intended that the world should come to the church to find Christ. Rather, He intended that the church move out into the world! The body of Christ was designed by God to be incarnate in the world, present in the world, visible in the marketplaces and public squares of the world. If the worldlings are able to see the body of Christ among them, ministering to them, challenging them, loving them, reaching them, they will understand that Jesus Christ is not dead and gone. He is here among them, in the form of ordinary believers.

Jesus Christ is active in the here and now. He's not off in some remote corner of the universe, not viewing the world through a telescope from heaven. He has not left His people here to struggle and flounder until He comes back again. Christ is alive and has been at work in human society for twenty centuries, just as He said He would be: "Lo, I am with you always, to the close of the age" (Matthew 28:20).

What, specifically, is the ministry of the body of Christ? Let us hear the answer from His own lips. It is found in one of the most dramatic and riveting scenes in the New Testament, as recorded in Luke 4. It is our Lord's own description of the ministry He came to accomplish on earth, whether in His physical body of flesh or in His corporate (but no less physical) body of the church. In Luke 4:16 we read, "And he came to Nazareth, where he had been brought up; and he went to the synagogue, as his custom was, on the sabbath day. And he stood up to read; and there was given to him the book of the prophet Isaiah."

Jesus began His ministry in the cities around the lake of Galilee with His headquarters in Capernaum. He then made an extensive journey into Jerusalem and Judea where He did many miracles. He soon gained a reputation throughout the land as a doer of good deeds and a worker of miracles. Word had come back to Nazareth, His hometown, of the strange and remarkable things this local youth had been doing. Now He has returned, and everyone in town knows that He will be in the synagogue on the Sabbath day. They all turn out to hear Him for they are anxiously hoping that He will do among them some of the miracles He has done in other cities.

But in the synagogue He calls for the scroll of the

prophet Isaiah, and—unrolling it to the proper place, which in our Old Testament is Isaiah 64—He reads the following passage: " 'The Spirit of the LORD is upon me, because he has anointed me to preach good news to the poor. He has sent me to proclaim release to the captives and recovering of sight to the blind, to set at liberty those who are oppressed, to proclaim the acceptable year of the LORD.' And he closed the book, and gave it back to the attendant, and sat down; and the eyes of all in the synagogue were fixed on him. And he began to say to them, 'Today this scripture has been fulfilled in your hearing' " (Luke 4:18–21).

There must have been many puzzled looks among the townspeople of Nazareth at this point. They must have said to themselves, "What does He mean? How could He say this Scripture was fulfilled among us when He has done no miracles in Nazareth at all?" Knowing this thought was in their hearts, Jesus went on to say: "Doubtless you will quote to me this proverb, 'Physician, heal yourself'; what we have heard you did at Capernaum, do here also in your own country" (Luke 4:23).

Then He went on to remind them that in the history of Israel, prophets were often not received in their own country by their own people. He cited the examples of Elijah and Elisha, who worked miracles of blessing for the Gentiles but did not do the same for any Israelites.

In what sense, therefore, did He mean that Isaiah's great prophecy of the Messiah had been fulfilled in Nazareth? He undoubtedly meant for them to see that the physical fulfillment of these predictions (opening blind eyes, healing the lame, and so forth) was not the sole intent of Scripture. The Messiah would indeed begin on that level in order to capture attention and evoke trust in Himself, but He would also fulfill the predictions at a deeper and more important level—the level of the human spirit. It is the healing of the human spirit God is really after, and it was on this level that the prophecy of Isaiah had been fulfilled in Nazareth.

The error of Israel

The majority in Nazareth had their expectations set on the physical alone. They wanted to be amazed by the sight of an honest-to-goodness physical miracle. They refused to accept the Lord's statement that ultimate fulfillment could be found only in the healing of the human spirit, not through awesome displays of divine power. When it became clear that He had no intention of working miracles, when they saw that He was claiming divine appointment as the Messiah without demonstrating any miraculous proof of His claim, they went berserk! The crowd turned into a lynch mob and attempted to push Him off the edge of the big cliff upon which Nazareth is built.

It has been often pointed out that the miracles that Jesus did are also *parables*. They make a vivid point on a physical level that symbolizes what Christ wants us to understand on the deeper level of the spirit. The mistake the Jews made during our Lord's ministry was that they would not accept the deep spiritual reality He tried to show them; instead, they were obsessed with seeing outward, physical signs and miracles. Paul said that this obsession with outward signs rather than inner reality continued to be the desire of the Jews even after the crucifixion; they would not believe the gospel without some kind of sign (see 1 Corinthians 1:22).

Those who hunger and thirst for physical miracles today are repeating this error of Israel. They constantly seek something visible, something spectacular, something clearly supernatural. It's a sad fact of human nature: We would rather see bread multiplied or water turned into wine than see the inner transformation of a human life! Somehow, walking on water seems like more of a miracle to us than the deliverance of a human soul from the darkness of sin! That is the error of Israel: Jesus made it clear to the people of Nazareth that the Messiah had come among them, fulfilling the ancient prophecies right before their eyes—but they didn't want to see liberated lives, they wanted to see a miracle show!

With this in mind, let's take a closer look at the words that Jesus read from the scroll of Isaiah, for this passage describes not only the physical fulfillment that occurred in the days of Jesus' physical life on earth, but also the fulfillment that will occur through you and me as Christians in the twentieth and twenty-first centuries.

You may recall that Jesus said of His disciples, "He who believes in me will also do the works that I do; and greater works than these will he do, because I go to the Father" (John 14:12). What are these "greater works"? From Jesus' perspective, it is clear that anything done in the realm of the spirit is greater than any miracle done in the body.

The physical raising of Lazarus from the tomb was truly amazing—yet it was next to nothing compared with the miracle of a sinner whose life has been completely redirected by the grace and love of God. All the bodily miracles and healings Jesus performed were just temporary cures. Lazarus, for example, eventually had to go through death again. But the work that Jesus does within the human heart and human soul is eternal, yielding blessing that goes on and on without end.

When Jesus went to the Father, He sent back the Holy Spirit, whose role it is to reproduce the life of Jesus in the believer. This is why Jesus is able to say that the church will do greater works than He Himself did upon the earth—because it is not really the church (or the individual Christian) doing those works. Rather, those works are being done by a risen, ascended Lord through the Holy Spirit, acting within the body of believers, the church.

There are four divisions in this work of the ministry that is described by Isaiah. These four divisions are introduced by the phrase, "The Spirit of the Lord is upon me, because he has anointed me" (Luke 4:18). What follows is a description of a Spirit-filled ministry. As Jesus was anointed by the Spirit for His ministry in His lifetime, so each believer must be filled with the Spirit for the work he is to do.

How can other people tell when the Spirit of God is at work in a certain person's life? Will it be by the display of some strange phenomenon, or by a miraculous manifestation? No, the Spirit-filled ministry will be the kind of ministry described by Isaiah. It will open spiritually blinded eyes, make the spiritually lame walk, free those spiritually held captive, and so forth. That is the purpose of a Spirit-filled life.

First, the work of the ministry is to evangelize: "He has anointed me to preach good news to the poor" (Luke 4:18). The first division of the work of the ministry is that the saints (ordinary Christians) are to declare the good news of God's activity in human history. That is evangelism. The good news is that God has not left the human race to struggle hopelessly in bewilderment, pain, and darkness. God has done something about the human condition. He has acted to deliver us from darkness to light through His Son, Jesus Christ. The Lord of the universe has gone to the cross and taken our sins upon Him. He hasn't merely spoken; He has acted. Through the resurrection, He has given men and women His own life, which empowers them to truly live. To tell this story is to preach the good news.

To whom is this good news to be preached? Clearly, it is not to be preached to the rich but to the poor! What does this mean? Surely it doesn't mean only those who are below the poverty line, and who are poor in the material things of this world! Aren't the rich and the wealthy to hear this good news too? Obviously, the prophecy goes beyond mere physical poverty, penetrating to the spiritual poverty of every man and woman.

Remember the first words of the greatest sermon ever preached, the Sermon on the Mount? It begins with a remarkable recipe for happiness, the Beatitudes. "Blessed [or happy] are the poor in spirit, for theirs is the kingdom of heaven." That is, happy is the one who has no spiritual resources left, and knows it. Happy is the person who does not have any standing before God, who does not have a long record of good works to rest on, who does not rely on a self-satisfied, self-righteous attitude. Happy is the person who comes to God and says, "Be merciful to me, a sinner!" God is then able to give to that person the kingdom of heaven.

Jesus never spent much time with the self-righteous and the self-sufficient. He preached to the poor in spirit. Don't waste time talking to people who think they have everything they need. Look for those who have nothing—but don't be fooled by appearances. Don't be misled by the fact that some pretend to have everything while underneath there is a searching, hungry heart. Some of the richest people in the world are also the emptiest. So get down to the heart-need and heart-poverty of that person. Preach the good news to the poor.

Release and recovery

The next assignment within the work of the ministry consists of two factors: (1) "to proclaim release to the captives" and (2) "recovering of sight to the blind" (Luke 4:18). Release and recovery of sight. Liberty and light.

Do you know any captives, any people who are bound by outlooks and attitudes that hold them in perpetual captivity? Do you know anyone who is struggling to free himself from hurtful habits which hold him in a vise-like grip? Do you know any people who are locked into a pattern of poisonous hate, or jealous bitterness, or possessive greed which they seem powerless to break? Are you such a person yourself? Then there is good news! Jesus Christ is able to set you free. He has done it for millions and He can do it for you.

Are there people who are blind today? Are there men and women who think they are doing the right thing and who mean to do the right thing but somehow it always turns out wrong? They are blind; they cannot see to the end of the paths they are on. Often they are perfectly sincere, honest people who hope they are doing right and are struggling along as well as they can. But nothing works out for them, and they end up stumbling blindly from one episode to another, deeper and deeper into difficulty. Aren't these people blind? Absolutely! They need the ministry Jesus announced in Luke 4:18—the recovery of sight to the blind.

This releasing and recovering ministry is the result of teaching the truth. Jesus said, "You will know the truth, and the truth will make you free" (John 8:32). Truth releases captives and restores sight. Truth doesn't mean telling people what they want to hear, but what they *need* to hear. Jesus said, "He who follows me will not walk in darkness, but will have the light of life" (John 8:12).

That is also the work of teaching: To disciple people and show them how to follow Jesus. Following Jesus means so much more than simply coming to church, singing hymns, and reciting creeds. It means obeying Him, even when every fiber of our being cries out to seek sin or selfishness. The work of teaching touches every compartment of our lives—our work, our family relationships, our friendships, our school relationships, the use of our spare time, our entertainment choices, our political involvement, our social concern, and on and on. Part of the work of the ministry is to teach men and women, boys and girls, how to lay hold of the power that releases them from captivity, so that they can boldly follow and obey the One who opens our eyes and leads us out of darkness and into the light.

A demonic element

The next element of a Spirit-filled ministry is to "set at liberty those who are oppressed" (Luke 4:18). At first glance this seems similar to proclaiming release to captives. It is true that the end result is the same: liberty. But the problem of oppression is a much deeper and more serious one than mere captivity. Oppression has a demonic element about it. It is more than mere tyranny, there is also a terrible cruelty involved. It results in a sense of burden, of dejection and depression, coupled with hopelessness.

A man once drove over 600 miles to tell me of a heavy burden that was oppressing him. For over a year he had been terribly affected by an attitude of hate toward another man who had done him a great injustice. He could not free himself of his bitterness and rancor. It began to trouble him so that he could not eat or sleep properly. On two or three occasions he had barely been able to restrain himself from committing murder. It was breaking him up, destroying his family, and threatening his own life. He was troubled by constant depression and despair.

We talked together, and I showed him the truth of the Scripture about his unforgiving spirit. I gently explained to him that he was poisoning his own life by his hatred, and that there could be no release until he was able to forgive the man who had offended him. He agreed to ask God for the grace to forgive, and we prayed together.

As we prayed, I watched his face and before my eyes a miracle—a genuine act of supernatural grace and power!—took place. I saw a man healed in front of my eyes. I saw a burden of bitterness and spiritual oppression lifted. I saw the poison of hate drain out of this man's heart as the love of Jesus Christ came flooding in. His whole attitude was visibly transformed, and he went home with a look of peace on his face and a sense of God's joy in his heart.

This is one example of the ministry of counseling and prayer that gives liberty to the oppressed. It doesn't take a pastor to do it; it can be accomplished by any Christian who knows the truth of the Word and has the faith to pray.

This man should not have had to drive 600 miles to find someone to help him. But unfortunately this ministry of prayer-counseling has been left for the professional counselor to handle. As a result, emotional and spiritual problems that could have been easily handled when they were small have been allowed to grow into tangled knots even professionals cannot always handle. Prayer is particularly effective in problems of this type. As Jesus once said of a demon-ridden boy, "This kind cannot be driven out by anything but prayer" (Mark 9:29).

The last element of the work of Christ's body in the world today is "to proclaim the acceptable year of the Lord" (Luke 4:19). This is one of the most remarkable statements in the Bible. If you will look up the original passage in Isaiah from which Jesus read, you will discover that there is a comma after the word *Lord.* The sentence is not complete at that point. In the original it goes on to say "and to declare the day of vengeance of our God" (Isaiah 61:1–2). The Lord Jesus did not read that part of the script. At the comma, He abruptly closed the book and handed it back, saying, "Today this scripture has been fulfilled in your hearing" (Luke 4:21).

Why did Jesus stop reading at that point? The answer is clear. He was implying that at that particular point in time, the rest of Isaiah's prophecy was *not* yet fulfilled. Today, as I write these words, that remainder of Isaiah's prophecy is *still* unfulfilled. That fulfillment could take place a second from now, a year from now, or a thousand years from now. The day of vengeance of our God awaits the second return of Jesus Christ. But the present age is the acceptable year of the Lord. Salvation is still possible.

When we proclaim this great fact, we explain and make clear what is happening in our world. We relieve the cold grip of fear that clutches at the hearts of thousands who get up every morning scared to death, not knowing what will happen to a world that has apparently gone quite mad. They open their newspapers or turn on CNN, and they see reports of terrorist attacks, bombings, nerve gas attacks, random murders, car-jackings, gang violence, riots, racial strife, political upheaval, wars and rumors of wars—and they are afraid that history is spinning out of control! They fear that God has lost command over human events—if He ever had control! They feel lost, like hopeless, helpless victims of inexorable forces far beyond their ability to understand, much less control.

The people of our world today desperately need to hear Christians proclaim to them the acceptable year of the Lord. They need to see from the Scriptures that God knows what He is doing in our day and age. They need to hear that God is *restraining* the forces of evil for a season, in order to permit the gospel to go out, while permitting a sufficient demonstration of the evil in man so that we will see our own sinfulness and helplessness, and recognize our need of God.

The Lord is governing human events according to His own purposes and His own timetable. The acceptable year of the Lord will go on only as long as God decrees—and then comes "the day of vengeance of our God"! But until the acceptable year of the Lord

ends and the terrible day of vengeance falls, no
human being can go beyond God's limits of restraint.

This, then, is the fourfold work of the ministry:
evangelizing, teaching, praying, and explaining the
times. This is the fourfold task of the church in the
world.

Is it relevant? Is it something people need,
something they are dying for, something they are
desperate to find? I will leave that for you to answer.
But if you see it as I do you will recognize that nothing
could be more exciting and fulfilling than to be
involved in ministry like this!

If you are a Christian, this is *your* ministry. To this
end, you have been equipped and prepared by God as
He has given you certain spiritual gifts. It is for this
purpose that you have within you the resurrection
power of the risen Lord from which to draw. The
pastor and evangelist, along with the apostles and
prophets, were never intended to do this ministry
alone. Rather, they have been given to help *you* carry
out this ministry yourself!

A normal part of life

You might say, "But when can I do this? After all, I
have to earn a living! I don't have time to go about
preaching and teaching!" There's an easy answer to that:
Do the work of the ministry God has given you wherever
you are. Do it at work. Do it in your home. Do it on the
golf course and the tennis court. Do it at the grocery
store and on the campus. This ministry is as natural and
normal a part of life as anything else you can do.

Obviously, the majority of Christians spend their
time doing the work of the work—and this is as it
should be. Not everyone is called to be a pastor, an

evangelist, or even a teacher. The major preoccupation of any person's life is his or her daily employment. But if Jesus Christ has no part in that, then He is Lord only of the margins of your life—of your leftover moments, your spare time.

Have you ever noticed that the really important figures of the New Testament are not the priests and monks. They are shepherds, fishermen, taxgatherers, soldiers, politicians, tentmakers, physicians, and carpenters! These are the ones who occupy the center of the stage. So it must be again today.

You can tell the good news of God at work around a water cooler in an office if the occasion is right. Or to another, over a lunch bucket. You can heal a hurting heart as you're going home in the carpool. You can teach the truth that liberates people over a cup of coffee in a kitchen or the back fence. You can pray the prayer of deliverance beside a sick bed. You can interject Christian insights into business transactions or governmental problems—and the insights you share may mean the difference between conflict and strife, hope and despair, or even heaven and hell for the person whose life you touch!

A Christian man once told me that he is a member of an urban renewal committee in San Francisco, responsible for clearing up slum areas in the city. At one of their meetings, the board considered setting up a new housing project in an area already crowded with tenements and flats. They faced the question of what to do about the people who would be displaced until the new housing was ready. There was a general feeling of, "That's their problem, let them take care of it."

But this Christian man said, "No, it is not their problem. It's our problem. We have no right to put in a housing project unless we face the responsibility of helping these people find some other place to live. Christian compassion can do nothing less!" He stood his ground, and because he spoke up at a critical moment, he made the committee face their responsibility and they eventually found a way to solve it.

In these perilous, polarized, apocalyptic times, it is easy to find an occasion to proclaim the acceptable year of the Lord. It is almost impossible to avoid it! You can quiet the fearful with a reassuring word of hope in almost any situation. All you need is a newspaper headline or a television commentary, and you have a wide open door to tell men of what God is doing in history and where He says it will all end.

We must never forget our Lord's story of the sheep and the goats, and the basis of His judgment between them. The whole point of the story is that Christians must not evade activities that involve them in the pain of the world. The hungry must be fed, the naked must be clothed, the sick must be visited, and those in prison must be helped to find the liberating Lord in the midst of their confinement.

God has given us all the gifts we need to carry out His eternal plan and strategy for the church. We dare not hide our gifts in the ground as the unfaithful servant did in the Lord's parable (see Matthew 25:14–30). When the acceptable year of the Lord has ended and we meet our Lord face to face, He will ask us for an accounting of how we have used our gifts in the body of Christ.

Now is the time we have to perform the tasks God has given us. Let us begin right *now* to put our gifts to work!

CHAPTER 10

KEEPING THE BODY HEALTHY

Josiah Henson was born into slavery in the American South. As a young boy, he saw members of his own family worked to death, beaten to death, and sold to other slave-owners. He was able to escape to the North, where he became a well-known public speaker and a leader in the movement to abolish slavery. Some years after the Civil War brought an end to slavery, Henson took a trip to England, where he gave a speech that was heard by the Archbishop of Canterbury. The Archbishop was impressed by the stately bearing and eloquent speaking ability of this former slave. Introducing himself to Henson after the conclusion of the black man's speech, the Archbishop asked what university Henson had attended.

"The University of Adversity," Henson replied.

Today, millions of people are unhappy students in the University of Adversity. This is a world filled with poverty, pain, oppression, injustice, and suffering. All of this adversity in the world is our opportunity for ministry. The work God has given us is directed toward a suffering and desperate world. Our Lord Jesus Christ requires every member of His body to accomplish this task effectively, with resurrection power, as God intended it to be done. This means that the members of the body must be spiritually healthy and vibrant with the life of Christ, who indwells all Christians through His Spirit.

No athlete spends all his time running races or playing the game for which he is trained. He must also spend many hours keeping himself in shape and developing his skills to a high degree. The same is true of the body of Christ.

The work of the ministry cannot be effectively carried out in a weak and unhealthy church—a church that is torn with internal pains, and wracked by spiritual diseases. So it is no surprise that the pattern of the Holy Spirit for the proper functioning of Christ's body includes not only a plan for "shaping up" the saints, but also a plan for keeping the saints healthy. Apostles, prophets, evangelists, and pastor-teachers exist not only to equip the members of the body to do ministry but also to build them up and support them in a mutual ministry to each other, so that the entire body will be vibrant, vital, and effective.

Unhealthy saints

Great damage has been done to the cause of Christ by unhealthy saints who attempted to carry out evangelistic or social ministry with great zeal but without true spiritual health. Burdened with unsolved problems in their own lives, often displaying unhealthy (and unrecognized) hypocrisy and prejudice, these Christians bring the body of Christ and the gospel of Christ into disrepute in the world. Their worship has become a dull, lifeless, predictable ritual. They display more reverence for their own religious traditions than for biblical truth. They talk about superficial matters around the coffeepot after church, and they call it "fellowship" and "Christian love"—even though there is little if any real involvement in each others' lives.

What is terribly missing in all too many churches is the experience of "body life"—that warm fellowship of Christian with Christian which the New Testament calls *koinonia*, and which was an essential part of early Christianity. The New Testament lays heavy emphasis upon the need for Christians to know each other, closely and intimately enough to be able to bear one another's burdens, confess faults one to another, encourage, exhort, and admonish one another; and minister to one another with the Word, song, and prayer. As we carry out the various "one another" ministries of New Testament-style body life, we will come to comprehend "with all saints," as the apostle Paul says, "what is the breadth and length and height and depth, and to know the love of Christ which surpasses knowledge" (Ephesians 3:18–19).

There are over fifty "one another" statements and commands in the New Testament, and these call us to a special kind of life together—what in this book we call "body life." These statements and commands are (in NIV):

- "Be at peace with each other" (Mark 9:50).
- "Wash one another's feet" (John 13:14).
- "Love one another" (John 13:34).
- "Love one another" (John 13:35).

- "Love each other" (John 15:12).
- "Love each other" (John 15:17).
- "Be devoted to one another in brotherly love" (Romans 12:10).
- "Honor one another above yourselves" (Romans 12:10).
- "Live in harmony with one another" (Romans 12:16).
- "Love one another" (Romans 13:8).
- "Stop passing judgment on one another" (Romans 14:13).
- "Accept one another, then, just as Christ accepted you" (Romans 15:7).
- "Instruct one another" (Romans 15:14).
- "Greet one another with a holy kiss" (Romans 16:16).
- "When you come together to eat, wait for each other" (1 Corinthians 11:33).
- "Have equal concern for each other" (1 Corinthians 12:25).
- "Greet one another with a holy kiss" (1 Corinthians 16:20).
- "Greet one another with a holy kiss" (2 Corinthians 13:12).
- "Serve one another in love" (Galatians 5:13).
- "If you keep on biting and devouring each other . . . you will be destroyed by each other" (Galatians 5:15).
- "Let us not become conceited, provoking and envying each other" (Galatians 5:26).
- "Carry each other's burdens" (Galatians 6:2).
- "Be patient, bearing with one another in love" (Ephesians 4:2).

- "Be kind and compassionate to one another" (Ephesians 4:32).
- "Forgiving each other" (Ephesians 4:32).
- "Speak to one another with psalms, hymns and spiritual songs" (Ephesians 5:19).
- "Submit to one another out of reverence for Christ" (Ephesians 5:21).
- "In humility consider others better than yourselves" (Philippians 2:3).
- "Do not lie to each other" (Colossians 3:9).
- "Bear with each other" (Colossians 3:13).
- "Forgive whatever grievances you may have against one another" (Colossians 3:13).
- "Teach [one another]" (Colossians 3:16).
- "Admonish one another" (Colossians 3:16).
- "Make your love increase and overflow for each other" (1 Thessalonians 3:12).
- "Love each other" (1 Thessalonians 4:9).
- "Encourage each other" (1 Thessalonians 4:18).
- "Encourage one another" (1 Thessalonians 5:11).
- "Build each other up" (1 Thessalonians 5:11).
- "Encourage one another daily" (Hebrews 3:13).
- "Spur one another on toward love and good deeds" (Hebrews 10:24).
- "Encourage one another" (Hebrews 10:25).
- "Do not slander one another" (James 4:11).
- "Don't grumble against each other" (James 5:9).
- "Confess your sins to each other" (James 5:16).
- "Pray for each other" (James 5:16).
- "Love one another deeply, from the heart" (1 Peter 1:22).
- "Live in harmony with one another" (1 Peter 3:8).
- "Love each other deeply" (1 Peter 4:8).

- "Offer hospitality to one another without grumbling" (1 Peter 4:9).
- "Each one should use whatever gift he has received to serve others"(1 Peter 4:10).
- "Clothe yourselves with humility toward one another (1 Peter 5:5).
- "Greet one another with a kiss of love" (1 Peter 5:14).
- "Love one another" (1 John 3:11).
- "Love one another" (1 John 3:23).
- "Love one another" (1 John 4:7).
- "Love one another" (1 John 4:11).
- "Love one another" (1 John 4:12).
- "Love one another" (2 John 5).

Obviously, the "one another" ministries in the body of Christ are extremely important to God, since He speaks of them so frequently in His Word. So the question we must ask ourselves is: "Where, in the usual, traditional church structure of the church is this kind of interchange possible? What provision is made by church leaders to encourage it and guide its expression through scriptural teaching and wise admonitions?"

In many churches, you can find some expression of body life taking place in private gatherings of Christians, usually in someone's home. But then, all too often, the church leaders find out about it, brand the gatherings as "divisive," and discourage body life from taking place! Authentic body life doesn't threaten the unity of the church—it is the very thing that the church is supposed to be about, according to the New Testament!

In the early church, as we see it described in the

New Testament, we see a rhythm of body life evident in the way Christians gathered together in homes to instruct one another, study and pray together, and share the ministry of spiritual gifts. Then they would go out into the world to let the warmth and glow of their love-filled lives overflow into a spontaneous Christian witness that drew love-starved pagans into the church like hungry children into candy store.

This was exactly in line with the exhortation of Jesus to His disciples: "A new commandment I give to you, that you love one another; even as I have loved you, that you also love one another. By this all men will know that you are my disciples, if you have love for one another" (John 13:34–35).

The early church relied upon a twofold witness as the means of reaching and impressing a cynical and unbelieving world: *kerygma* (proclamation) and *koinonia* (fellowship). It was the combination of these two that made the church's witness so powerful and effective. "In the mouth of two or three witnesses shall every word be established" (Matthew 18:16 KJV). Pagans could easily shrug off the proclamation as simply another "teaching" among many; but they found it much more difficult to reject the evidence of *koinonia*. The concern of Christians for each other, and the way they shared their lives in the same great family of God, left the pagan world craving and envying this new experience called *koinonia*. It prompted the much-quoted remark of a pagan writer: "How these Christians love one another!"

The present-day church has managed to do away with true New Testament *koinonia* almost completely, reducing the witness of the church to proclamation (*kerygma*) alone. It has thus succeeded in doing two things simultaneously: removing the major safeguard to the health of the church from within, and greatly weakening its effective witness before the world without. It is little wonder, therefore, that the church has fallen on evil days and is regarded as irrelevant and useless by so many in the world.

Fulfilling Christ's law

It is time to take seriously again certain admonitions of Scripture that have somehow been passed over lightly, even by so-called Bible-believing Christians. Let's take a closer look at some of the "one another" passages that call us to a body life way of living.

Take, for instance, this strong word from Galatians 6:2: "Bear one another's burdens, and so fulfill the law of Christ." Note that the apostle indicates that this is the way by which the fundamental law of the Christian life is fulfilled. That law is the "new commandment" of Jesus: "love one another" (John 13:34). The law of love is fulfilled only by bearing one another's burdens. But how can we bear each other's burdens if we don't know what those burdens are? Some way of sharing these burdens with others is obviously called for.

Koinoinia calls for honesty and openness with other Christians, and a mutual recognition that it is neither abnormal nor unspiritual to have burdens and problems in our day-to-day Christian experience. Somehow the masks have to come off. The façades that say "everything is all right" when everything is anything but right have to fall. Often this can best be done in small groups, meeting in homes—though we have found at Peninsula Bible Church that the sharing of burdens and the experience of loving, nonjudgmental acceptance and caring can take place in larger meetings, including worship services. Many people fear rejection or giving rise to scandal in such settings, yet we have found that body life can take place in safety, even in a gathering of a thousand people or more. (See chapter 12 for a complete discussion and updating of body life at Peninsula Bible Church.)

Bearing one another's burdens at the very least means to uphold one another in prayer. It also means to be willing to spend time with another person so that you can thoroughly understand that person's feelings and problems. It means committing yourself to an authentic effort to relieve that person's pressures or discouragement, offering intense prayer, practical help, or wise counsel, not just a superficial word of "I'll pray for you."

Many Christians see other Christians in need and think, "Well, that's what the welfare department is for," or, "That's what unemployment insurance is for," or, "That's why I pay taxes." But Christians should never transfer their biblical "one another" responsibilities to an unfeeling, non-Christian government program or bureaucracy. Yes, help from government sources can be welcomed and utilized when needs arise, as can assistance from charitable agencies such as the Salvation Army, the Red Cross, or the United Way. But none of these agencies is a substitute for genuine Christian caring, expressed through an act of love, an affirming embrace, a word of encouragement, or a time of prayer.

Another direct exhortation from the Word is that of James 5:16: "Confess your sins to one another, and pray for one another, that you may be healed." Confessing faults means to admit weaknesses and to acknowledge failures in our Christian lives. It is often difficult to get Christians to do this, despite the clear counsel of God's Word. It goes against the grain to give an image of oneself that is anything less than perfect. Many Christians fear that they will be rejected by others if they admit to any faults. But nothing could be more destructive to authentic Christian *koinonia* and body life than the common practice today of pretending not to have any problems.

Many Christian families are suffering with conflict, sickness, dysfunctional behavior, addictions, pain, employment problems, and the like—yet those same families project an image of warm-fuzzy, idyllic Christian perfection. To make matters worse, this tragic conspiracy of silence is regarded as the "Christian" thing to do, and the hypocrisy it presents to the outside world is considered a necessary part of a family's "witness." How helpful and healing it would be if our Christian families—and our collective church family—would honestly confess the pain and problems that exist so that restoration can take place. It is especially helpful if husbands and fathers—who have the spiritual leadership role in Christian families—would honestly admit in a gathering of fellow Christians that they struggle and hurt, so that prayers and counsel can be offered.

This kind of honesty would also be helpful and healing to the individual family members. People need to hear that other Christians have the same kinds of problems. They need to hear other Christians say, "I really admire your honesty in sharing this issue, and your courage in taking this step toward healing." They need to have their issues and problems mirrored back to them by other believers, so that they can see their own problems more clearly. They need to receive the counsel and prayers of other believers, so that the healing power of God can be released in their midst.

Frederick the Great, King of Prussia during the mid-1700s, once toured a Berlin prison. As he entered one large, lower dungeon of the prison, a group of prisoners—about a dozen in all—fell on their knees before him. "Have mercy on us, your majesty!" they pleaded. "We are innocent! We have been falsely imprisoned!"

"*All* of you are innocent?" asked the king, surprised.

"Yes!" they insisted, every last man.

Then King Frederick noticed a man who stood off by himself in a dark corner of the dungeon. "You there!" said the king. "Why are you in this prison?"

"I was convicted of armed robbery, your majesty."

"Are you guilty?"

The man hung his head. "Yes, your majesty. Guilty and ashamed. I deserve to be in this place."

"Guard!" King Frederick called. "Guard! See that man in the corner? Take him out of here and release him at once!" Then, indicating the dozen men who had claimed to be unjustly imprisoned, he said, "I will not have these fine, innocent men corrupted by one guilty wretch!"

You and I are like that guilty prisoner. It is not our façade of goodness, but *the honest confession* of our sin that sets us free! "Confess your faults to one another," says James 5:16, "and pray for one another, that you may be healed. The prayer of a righteous man has great power in its effects."

Restoration of *koinonia*

It's significant that whenever spiritual awakenings have occurred throughout Christian history, they have always been accompanied by a restoration of *koinonia*-fellowship, including the confession of faults, and the bearing of one another's burdens. During the Wesleyan awakening in eighteenth-century England, the great evangelist George Whitefield wrote to his converts:

> My brethren . . . let us plainly and freely tell one another what God has done for our souls. To this end you would do well, as others have done, to form yourselves into little companies of four or five each, and meet once a week to tell each other what is in your hearts; that you may then also pray for and comfort each other as need shall require. None but those who have experienced it can tell the unspeakable advantages of such a union and communion of souls. . . .
>
> None I think that truly loves his own soul, and his brethren as himself, will be shy of opening his heart, in order to have their advice, reproof, admonition, and prayers, as occasions require. A sincere person will esteem it one of the greatest blessings.[1]

When this kind of sharing and burden bearing takes place in a church, the elders and pastors will be relieved of much of the counseling and crisis intervention burden they might otherwise be forced to do. Many spiritual, emotional, and even mental problems could be solved at the beginning if caring Christians would accept their biblical responsibility to show genuine Christian love and concern for their brothers and sisters in the body. In fact, modern techniques of group therapy are built on this basic body life principle that had its beginnings in the early church.

Obviously there are certain matters that should not be voiced in an open meeting—matters of an intimate or scandalous nature, for example. Some types of sharing should be done privately between only two or three individuals who are trustworthy and mature in their insights. But no Christian should bear a heavy burden alone. Those with the gift of encouragement should make themselves available to others for this ministry, and any who appear withdrawn, troubled, or downcast should be gently encouraged to unload their burden. The gift of a listening ear and an understanding heart is sometimes the greatest gift one Christian can give another.

The essential admonition in Scripture regarding the ministry of building up and edifying one another in the body of Christ is Ephesians 4:15: "speaking the truth in love." In the Greek, the verb *speaking* does not appear. More literally, this verse says simply "truthing in love." It conveys a sense not merely of speaking the truth but demonstrating the truth through our lifestyle and behavior in every area of life.

Unloving silence

Most of us tend to shy away from confrontational situations—and understandably so. Confrontation is unpleasant. But in the church, confrontation is sometimes necessary for the health of the church. This is an area where Christians often fail one another, and allow the body of Christ to become unhealthy and ineffective.

If someone has an unpleasant or irritating habit, we're quick enough to discuss it with others—but are we willing to say something directly to that person? If we do, it is usually only when we have been angered or annoyed to the point of unloading on that person in a destructive way! Why are we so reluctant to deal with our complaints and objections face to face? We tell ourselves, "I don't want to hurt his feelings," or, "I don't want to make her feel bad." But we're just fooling ourselves.

The fact is, we don't want to pay the price of "speaking the truth in love." We don't want to risk having to deal with an unpleasant or uncomfortable situation. We don't want to have to deal with that other person's tears, anger, or resistance. It's so much easier to simply gripe behind that person's back rather than to lovingly confront their sin or flaw. The problem: In our silence and timidity, we do that person a great deal of harm. We condemn that person to go on offending others and suffering rejection, when we could allow God to use us to produce positive change in that person's life! Worst of all: we "baptize" our silence, convincing ourselves that our cowardly avoidance of confrontation is actually a mark of "Christian love."

Christians who have lived in an authentic atmosphere of *koinonia* and body life will tell you: They are grateful beyond words that another Christian has cared enough to illuminate their blind spot, and to help them become more mature and more like Jesus Christ. Confrontation is painful and unpleasant for everyone involved—but it is the pain of health-giving surgery, not the pain of a damaging injury. "Faithful are the wounds of a friend," says Proverbs 27:6.

Of course, confrontation must always be undertaken in a spirit of humility and gentleness, in the full knowledge that we ourselves are vulnerable to errors and blind spots, and someday it will be our turn to be confronted. There are, of course, a few people in almost every church who love to confront others, who arrogantly take it upon themselves to run other people's lives. These are the Diotrephes-type church bosses—and we must continually purify our motives to make sure we don't take prideful pleasure in "setting other Christians straight." We must take seriously the words of Galatians 6:1: "Brethren, if a man is overtaken in any trespass, you who are spiritual should restore him in a spirit of gentleness. Look to yourself, lest you too be tempted."

This is the ministry of washing one another's feet, which Jesus said was absolutely necessary among His disciples: "If I then, your Lord and Teacher, have washed your feet, you also ought to wash one another's feet. For I have given you an example, that you also should do as I have done to you" (John 13:14–15). That He meant this to be taken symbolically and not literally is seen in His words, "What I am doing you do not know now, but afterward you will understand" (John 13:7).

One can never perform the ministry of foot-washing without taking the place of a servant as our Lord did. And—as Dr. H. A. Ironside used to say—it helps to be careful of the temperature of the water we use! Some come to wash the feet of others with icy cold water, saying, "Stick your feet in here!" Their cold, forbidding attitude arouses only resentment. Others are so angry and upset within themselves that they offer to wash the feet of other people in boiling water, right off the stove! The only way to truly serve others by washing their feet is to come with pleasingly warm water, making the unpleasant task of foot-washing as pleasurable as possible. The one thing we must *not* do is to turn away and leave the offending person unrestored and unhelped.

A healthy body is necessary to perform effective work. To attempt evangelism while the body of Christ is sick and afflicted is worse than useless. It is not difficult to keep a body of Christians healthy and vital if the members of that body—and especially the leaders—are diligent to bear one another's burdens, confess their faults to one another, instruct one another, and admonish one another in love, by means of the Word of God.

As we work to maintain the health and vitality of the church, we enable the body to become all God designed it to be: a church "in splendor, without spot or wrinkle or any such thing" (Ephesians 5:27).

CHAPTER 11

THE GOAL IS MATURITY

What is God doing through the church? What is He after? What is the end of it all?

Now we come to Ephesians 4:13–16, where we find Paul's great statement of the end and goal of all God's far-flung strategy for the human race. God's goal, says the apostle, is for us to "attain to the unity of the faith and of the knowledge of the Son of God, to mature manhood, to the measure of the stature of the fullness of Christ; so that we may no longer be children, tossed to and fro and carried about with every wind of doctrine, by the cunning of men, by their craftiness in deceitful wiles. Rather, speaking the truth in love, we are to grow up in every way into him who is the head, into Christ, from whom the whole body, joined and knit together by every joint with which it is supplied, when each part is working properly, makes bodily growth and upbuilds itself in love" (Ephesians 4:13–16).

Twice in this great passage, the apostle gives us the ultimate goal of the life of faith. It is the measuring stick by which we can judge our progress as Christians. In verse 13 he says it is "the measure of the stature of the fullness of Christ." And in verse 15 he urges us to "grow up in every way into him who is the head, into Christ." He puts it also in a most descriptive phrase, "mature manhood"! That means God wants you and me to fulfill our humanity, the design for us that God intended when He created the first man and the first woman.

It is important to realize that, according to this passage in Ephesians, the supreme purpose of the church is *not* the evangelization of the world. The Great Commission is often held up to us as the supreme aim and purpose of the church, and it is certainly a crucial and essential task. Jesus has clearly sent us out to preach the gospel to every creature. But the Great Commission is not God's supreme and ultimate goal. Romans 8:29 tells us that God's ultimate plan for us is that we be "conformed to the image of his Son." Evangelization is a means of bringing people into a relationship with God, so that God's ultimate goal for them— Christlikeness—can be achieved in their lives.

Nor does Paul say anything here about accomplishing world peace and universal justice. He does not say the church will ultimately introduce the millennium. We may well believe in the great vision of the prophets that there is a day coming when peace shall reign on the earth and men shall beat their swords into plowshares and make war no more. One day righteousness *shall* prevail over all the earth and all of today's headlines of injustice, tragedy, war, mass murder, terrorism, crime, racism, and hate will be forgotten. But that is not the great and final purpose for the existence of the church.

God's overarching goal is to produce men and

women who demonstrate the character qualities of Jesus Christ. God does not want a church filled with white-robed saints. He does not want a church filled with theological authorities or cultured clergyman. He wants a church filled with ordinary men and women who exemplify the extraordinary integrity, temperament, wholeness, compassion, individuality, boldness, righteousness, earnestness, love, forgiveness, selflessness, and faithfulness of Jesus Christ!

Our heart's desire

Deep in your own heart, isn't that what you truly desire? You want to be a whole person, a complete human being. You want to discover and fulfill all that God has built into you. The proof that this is deep in every human heart is a fact psychologists confirm when they explain that we all have a mental image of ourselves that approaches, in some considerable degree, our ideal of humanity. We tend to think of ourselves as being much more mature than we really are. The power of human self-deception is almost limitless. Even in those times when we try to be as ruthlessly, brutally honest as we can possibly be with ourselves, denial and self-deception rise up to prevent us from feeling the full pain of the truth.

We may say, "I'm a stubborn, foolish, selfish person"—but let someone *agree* with us at that point and we blow up! "What do you mean?" we say. "How dare you say such a thing about me!" It's all because we long to fulfill our humanity, to be the kind of idealized persons that God originally designed us to be.

And that is what the church is all about. It is the vehicle designed by God to achieve mature humanity—a humanity exactly like that which was exemplified by the life of Jesus Christ. We have now come full circle, for this is where the apostle began: the church is to fulfill its calling—the calling of demonstrating to the world a new character, a spirit of lowliness, love, and unity, coupled with resurrection power, proving that the church is a body inhabited and directed by God Himself!

As we examine the issue of Christlike maturity, we should distinguish between two words that are frequently used today: *spirituality* and *maturity*. Though related, they are not the same thing.

We can liken the spiritual life to the physical life of an individual. In this analogy, then, spirituality would be the counterpart of physical health. To be spiritual is to have good spiritual health. It involves keeping the mind and the will centered on the revelations of God and on the viewpoint of God about life, resulting in a habit of spiritual thinking that expects God to work in and through normal human activities.

Now, I grant that no one does this very well at first. Spirituality is a condition of openness to the Spirit of God as well as responsiveness to the will of God as it is made clear to us. In a person's early Christian life, he obviously does not understand a great deal about the will of God. Much of the revealed truth of the Word is unknown to him at this early stage of his spiritual development. Even what he is able to read in the Bible is often mysterious and difficult to understand. He lacks maturity—yet a lack of maturity doesn't necessarily mean a lack of spirituality!

A Christian can be very spiritual right from the beginning of his Christian experience. In fact, spiritual health is essential to the new Christian so that he can grow and lay hold of the knowledge of the Word. Just as a child needs bodily health to move from infancy to adulthood, so a Christian needs spiritual health in order to move from an infant faith to mature Christian character. If a child's health fades, his maturity is threatened; healthy children move on to maturity. The same is true in the spiritual realm. If spirituality—the habit of spiritual thinking and behavior—is maintained as a condition of life, then maturity will ultimately result.

A relative concept

Having defined *spirituality*, we next examine what *maturity* means. I would define maturity as the full range of understanding of the knowledge and will of God, increasing in depth as a Christian grows older. It includes the entire range of experience to which a Christian is subjected. If you think of it this way, you can see immediately that maturity must be considered as a relative concept.

We might say that this person is "very mature" or that person is "immature," but what is the objective standard we are using to arrive at such an assessment? The fact is, we are not able to apply a truly objective standard. The only truly objective standard is Christ Himself, and our knowledge of Him is imperfect because we are fallible and limited. So when we use the term *mature*, we are unconsciously applying a standard that really means something like "compared with the average Christian."

The apostle Paul uses this term *mature*—or, as it is sometimes translated in the Scriptures, *perfect*—in both a relative and an absolute sense. In Philippians 3:12, for instance, he says, "Not that I have already obtained this or am already perfect." He acknowledges his realization that he has not achieved perfection which, of course, only Jesus Christ Himself has ever manifested.

But later in the same passage, the apostle says, "Let those of us who are mature [or perfect] be thus minded" (3:15). Here he speaks of himself, as well as others around him, as being mature. This is obviously the relative use of the term and means a greater maturity than is usually found in the church.

The apostle John has given us a helpful way to gauge various levels of maturity. In 1 John 2:12, he writes, "I am writing to you, little children, because your sins are forgiven for his sake. I am writing to you, fathers, because you know him who is from the beginning. I am writing to you, young men, because you have overcome the evil one." When he speaks of certain Christians as little children, the fact that characterizes them is that they know their sins are forgiven. Certainly that is the first thing a new Christian learns. Therefore, as long as they are celebrating (and quite properly so!) in that stage of understanding, glorying in the fact that their sins are forgiven, they can be lovingly classified as "little children."

John doesn't mean, of course, that they are to forsake their initial excitement over having their sins forgiven. On the contrary, they should have a continually *increasing* awareness of the forgiveness of sin as they go through life. He simply means that a focus on the joy of being forgiven marks the *initial* stage of the Christian life—not maturity.

Then he says, "I am writing to you, fathers, because you know him who is from the beginning." For a long time, I thought John was referring to God the Father, the one who is from the beginning. But thinking back to the way he opens the letter, I began to realize that this is really a reference to the Son: "That which was from the beginning, which we have heard, which we have seen with our eyes, which we have looked upon and touched with our hands, concerning the word of life" (1 John 1:1). Here he is obviously referring to the Lord Jesus Himself.

The mark of a spiritual father, then, is a deep and thorough understanding of the deity and the humanity of Jesus, the fullness of the revelation that has come to us through the Son. It is to have a deep sense of acquaintanceship with Him, of closeness to Him, of having walked with Him through much of life. Out of that closeness comes a clarity of understanding of Jesus' words to such a degree that there is a grasp of the great doctrines which He came to reveal. This level of maturity means to display an understanding and a manifestation of the same characteristics that Jesus consistently manifested: compassion, tolerance, patience, justice, and forgiveness. Only a long-term relationship with the Son of God can produce such qualities.

Finally, the young men are characterized as having overcome the evil one, as having reached a stage of maturity where there is an understanding and a practice of the way to resist temptation. Temptation, of course, comes from the evil one and the ability to handle temptation is a mark of a maturing individual, one who knows how to distinguish between good and evil. As the writer of Hebrews puts it, "Solid food is for the mature, for those who have their faculties trained by practice to distinguish good from evil" (Hebrews 5:14).

The kind of person who is overcoming the wicked one is able to see evil as evil (even when it looks good!) by the revelation of the Scriptures and by the understanding given by the Spirit.

Amplified version

Now the apostle John goes on to repeat these three statements to the "children," "fathers," and "young men" of the church, and he adds a few statements to amplify his thought. He says, "I write to you, children, because you know the Father." That, of course, is how they came to forgiveness of sin. They came into an awareness of the fatherhood of God by faith in Jesus Christ, when God immediately became a father to them. The two things that mark the beginning experience of a Christian, then, are that wonderful sense of sins having been forgiven and of belonging to a family under God the Father.

Then he says again, "I write to you, fathers, because you know him who was from the beginning." No change there; it simply cannot be improved upon. The mark of a mature individual is that this individual knows Jesus Christ, that he or she is growing continually in an understanding of His teachings (both directly and through His apostles), and that he or she demonstrates a growing evidence that the Spirit of God is reproducing Christ's character within.

Now John says, "I write to you, young men, because you are strong, and the word of God abides in you, and you have overcome the evil one." There he gives us a little further insight into how the young men overcome the evil one. They are strong—strong in spirit, that is—and they are responsive to what they're learning. Furthermore, the Word of God abides in them; it is the truth they are learning that makes them strong. They are functional, able to be useful in the kingdom of God. This passage in John's letter illuminates the process of growth; maturity does not happen all at once.

Returning to Ephesians 4, in verse 15, Paul says, "We are to grow up in every way . . . into Christ." Then again, in the latter part of verse 16, he says the body "makes bodily growth and upbuilds itself in love." Growth is God's method. It is a process, and it does not happen overnight. It is a matter that requires time.

This is a crucially important principle to understand. I know many Christians who are greatly disturbed when, having become Christians, they do not find themselves suddenly and remarkably transformed into angelic creatures. They still find much of the old life very much present. The old attitudes are still tugging and even controlling their behavior. They do not know what to make of this, and many are tempted to believe that it is a sign they are not true Christians at all. If their faith is in Christ, then they are Christians, period. But they need to learn that a process of growth must follow and it requires time for growth to occur.

This necessity for growth is why the Scriptures warn against putting a new, spiritually young Christian into a position of authority. He simply has not had enough experience in the things of the Lord to be able to carry that burden of responsibility. The growth of his intellectual knowledge of Christian doctrine may have been most rapid and impressive, but knowledge alone does not make a man of God. In fact, time alone is no guarantee of growth! But if the factors that make for growth are present, then growth will occur—if we are patient, persistent, and faithful to God.

How do you grow?

New Christians should also understand that growth does not come by trying. As Jesus pointed out, you cannot add an inch to your stature by thinking. You cannot say, "Now I am going to try to grow." Children would grow much faster than they do if that would work! But it doesn't.

How, then, do you grow? You must make sure that the factors that enhance and encourage spiritual growth are present. If they are, growth will occur of itself, naturally and unforced. We have already examined many of these factors, but they are summarized by the apostle Paul in this twofold way: increasing in (1) "the unity of the faith" and (2) "the knowledge of the Son of God." These, he says, will lead to mature manhood, "the measure of the stature of the fullness of Christ" (Ephesians 4:13).

The *unity of the faith* is the shared understanding, in the church, of the great truths revealed in the Scriptures. Though the Scriptures are unchanging, new light is continually issuing forth from them through individual prophets and teachers who are given these new insights by the Holy Spirit. But then they must be shared widely in the body or no new truth is given. New Christians grow when they exert themselves to understand the Scriptures with the help of the teachers and leaders who make themselves available to them within the body of Christ. No growth toward wholeness and perfection can occur without this increase in the unity of the faith through the understanding of Christian doctrine.

But it must also be accompanied by an increase in the *knowledge of the Son of God.* This refers to experience, to a growing encounter with the Lord Jesus Himself, so that we come to know Him more and more—not just know about God, but *knowing God*, directly and personally. That, too, is necessary for maturity. It is the other factor that makes growth possible.

This encounter occurs when the knowledge of the faith (hearing) is put into practice (doing). Hearing and doing go hand in hand. You cannot *know* Jesus Christ until you *follow* Him. The disciples had an acquaintance with Jesus Christ before they became His disciples. That is obvious from the Gospel records. But they never *knew* Him until they left everything and followed Him. It is here that we are particularly helped by the prayers and concern of the other members of the body. In our relationships with one another, our experience of the Lord who lives within us is deepened and enlarged. As Jesus said when He revealed the standard of judgment for the last day, "Inasmuch as ye have done it unto one of the least of these my brethren, ye have done it unto me" (Matthew 25:40 KJV).

Since growth is a matter of knowledge plus obedience plus time, we do not need to be discouraged if we find that we are not yet completely like Christ. Some years ago, a button could be seen on the lapels of many Christians. The button read:

P B P G I N T W M Y

When you asked that person, "What do those letters stand for?" he or she would reply, "Please Be Patient, God Is Not Through With Me Yet."

This is a great truth! It is not a statement of an unwillingness to change, but of a recognition that change takes time—but it *is* taking place! The proper attitude for a healthy Christian is an eagerness to grow.

I once asked a boy how old he was. Quick as a flash he said, "I'm twelve, going on thirteen, but soon to be fourteen." That's the kind of eagerness for maturity we *all* should have! We do not need to ask ourselves, "Am I mature? Am I completely like Christ?" Instead, we should ask ourselves, "Am I on the way? Is there progress? Am I growing in the right direction?"

No longer children

The apostle Paul gives us two practical means by which we may measure our growth toward full maturity. One is negative and the other is positive. He puts it negatively first: "So that we may no longer be children, tossed to and fro and carried about with every wind of doctrine, by the cunning of men, by their craftiness in deceitful wiles" (Ephesians 4:14).

If you wish to know whether you are growing or not, do not measure yourself by comparison with someone else. That will tell you nothing. Instead, ask yourself, "Am I moving away from childish attitudes? Am I forsaking infantile behavior? Am I still governed by childish reactions and outbursts?" That is the first way to measure your degree of maturity.

The Scriptures often exhort us to be child*like*, but never to be child*ish*. These are two very different things! Childlikeness is that refreshing simplicity of faith which believes God and acts without questioning. But childishness is described here by the apostle as instability and naivete.

Children are notoriously fickle. Their attention span is short. You cannot interest them in one thing very long, because they quickly turn to something else. They are unstable, tossed to and fro, and carried about by every changing circumstance. This is the invariable mark of an immature believer in Christ—and an immature believer may be either brand-new in the faith or long-time believer who is undeveloped in his Christian experience. There are fads and fashions in the religious life, and immature Christians are forever riding the crest of some new fad. They are always running after the newest book or teacher, extolling them as the ultimate answer to spiritual need. This instability and "short spiritual attention span" are marks of immaturity. They do not seem to understand that the oldest book, the oldest teacher, is the most exciting of all: the Bible!

Immaturity and vacillation can be seen in the realm of actions as well. The childish Christian manifests himself by unfaithfulness and undependability. Many times new Christians will undertake some ministry or task with great eagerness and interest. But it is not very long before their interest wanes and they run out of gas. Soon they become discouraged, or fail to show up altogether! Unreliability can easily be forgiven in new Christians, but when it is manifested by those who have been Christians for many years it is much harder to bear. With experience and maturity in the Christian life comes visible evidence, as described by the apostle Paul—and that evidence includes faithfulness: "But the fruit of the Spirit is love, joy, peace, patience, kindness, goodness, faithfulness, gentleness, self-control" (Galatians 5:22–23).

A second mark of childishness is to be undiscerning and naive. Have you ever noticed how children are often unaware of danger? They may play in dangerous situations and be totally unaware that anything is threatening them. In the same way, young

Christians are often caught by "the cunning of men, by their craftiness in deceitful wiles" (Ephesians 4:14). This is an apt description of the many cultists, religious racketeers, charlatans, false prophets and teachers, and manipulative religious leaders who abound in our day. They trap many immature Christians (including many spiritually immature Christians who are chronologically "mature") with their teachings that sound so right and enticing.

One of the surest signs of immaturity is a confident, arrogant certainty, "I'm established, I will never fall, I will never forsake the Lord or be deceived." It was childish immaturity in the faith that led Peter to say, just prior to the crucifixion, "Lord, others may deny You, these other disciples of Yours may fall away, but there is one man You can count on, and that's me!"

But the Lord said, "Thank you, Peter, but before the rooster crows twice you will have denied me three times" (see Mark 14:29–30). That is how much Peter's well-intentioned zeal, rooted in spiritual immaturity, was worth!

Reluctance to move

A third mark of childishness is an unwillingness to move on to lay hold of the life and power of God which results in righteous behavior. Such a person clings instead to the initial phase of life as a baby Christian. The writer to the Hebrews puts it this way: "For though by this time you ought to be teachers"— and there, it seems to me, is a measuring mark of maturity: every mature Christian ought to be able to teach to some degree, whether or not they have a special gift of teaching—"you need someone to

teach you again the first principles of God's word"
(Hebrews 5:12).

Those first principles are the limited understanding of the Word attained by new Christians or
immature believers. He describes this as milk: "You
need milk, not solid food; for every one who lives on
milk is unskilled in the word of righteousness, for he is
a child" (verse 13).

I like to think of righteousness in terms of the
modern concept of "worth." Someone who is unright-
eous in behavior is always so because he is not resting
upon a true basis of worth imparted to him as a gift, the
gift of righteousness by faith in Jesus Christ. As he grows
in the knowledge of righteousness and in the awareness
of his full acceptance before God, he is increasingly
delivered from the need to produce a feeling of
acceptance before God by works, by activities, by self-
righteousness, or by other false means.

The writer to the Hebrews then goes on to say in
chapter 5, "But solid food"—that is, the "word of
righteousness"—"is for the mature, for those who have
their faculties trained by practice to distinguish good
from evil" (verse 14).

Now in Hebrews 6, which begins with the word
therefore, there is a tie with what the writer has just said
in the previous chapter. We tend to miss this because
of the unfortunate interjection of the chapter break.
His word really goes on and says, "Therefore let us
leave the elementary doctrines of Christ." These are
doctrines with which a new believer, still immature
and understandably so, would be concerned. He lists
them now: "not laying again a foundation of
repentance from dead works. . . ." Our works cannot
save us; only faith in the work Jesus did on the cross

can save. This is an elementary doctrine, the first truth that gives us admittance into the kingdom. Repentance from trying to save ourselves by our own works is the beginning of Christian faith.

The writer of Hebrews goes on to list other elementary issues of the faith: "faith toward God, with instruction about ablutions [rites such as baptism, the Lord's Supper, and so forth], the laying on of hands, the resurrection of the dead, and eternal judgment" (Hebrews 6:1–2). Now all these things are *initial* stages, relating to the realm of children growing and learning the truth. It is a terrible thing for those who have been Christians for years to be still involved heavily, on an emotional level, with these elementary doctrines. They are like cases of arrested development, like children with a tragic glandular disorder that prevents them from growing.

God wants us to leave these things and go on to maturity; that is, to the word of righteousness which is the solid food that ought to occupy the thoughts of the spiritually mature. The point is, a mature (or maturing) Christian ought to be increasingly concerned with manifesting the character of Christ through obedience to the Word of God.

Now the question arises: What about you? How much have you grown? Are you moving away from these childish attributes of instability and over-confidence? Are you growing in the faith and in the knowledge of the Son of God?

Growth does not always occur at a constant speed. The Scriptures indicate that it is discernible in stages. Did you ever watch a child growing? Parents know that growth follows a physical pattern in definite stages.

A friend told me recently about his fourteen-year-old

boy and the way he was shooting up into manhood. He had grown a foot taller in the last year. The father said that for fourteen years he had been able to wear a certain size shoe without rivalry, but his son had suddenly developed the same size foot—and now he found his son was constantly borrowing his shoes! He concluded with a relieved sigh, "The last time we bought shoes for that boy, his feet had grown beyond mine. So now I am safe again."

Whether in the spiritual realm or the physical realm, that is how growth takes place: by stages.

We enter the Christian life as spiritual babies and may grow quite rapidly at first. Then for a while we may resist the great principles that make for Christian development. We may be surprised to learn that God intends to do something quite different with us than we thought He would when we first became Christians. We resist these changes and do not like the way He deals with us at times, so growth slows down. But finally He brings us to the place where we give in and accept the radical principles and give ourselves to understanding them.

Then we experience a new surge of growth. We feel we have at last overcome our hot tempers or our passionate natures, and we think we have learned to be easygoing, friendly, happy individuals. We give up our bitter-ness, our grudges, our jealousy, and other ugly aspects of our old, immature nature. Then, to our dismay, we are put with the wrong person or into a sudden crisis, and the old garbage that we thought was completely washed out of us comes spewing forth again! We sag with discouragement and go to the Lord and say, "What's the matter with me, Lord? Why am I still so immature?"

Have you ever felt that way? I have, many times. But God is not through with us yet! We gradually learn how deceitful the flesh is and how it resists detection. Looking back we can see that we too are following the stages outlined by the apostle John—stages which are *perfectly normal* to Christian growth: "little children," then "young men," and finally "fathers."

We may come into a relative degree of maturity within a few years of our conversion, but we shall be engaged in the process of growth as long as we live in these earthly bodies. After all, it takes God years to grow an oak tree, but He can grow a squash in three months and a radish in a few weeks! The world has seen enough of Christian squashes and radishes. We need more strong, patient, mature oak trees!

But there is a second way by which we can measure our growth. Negatively we can mark the distance we have moved from childish attitudes, but there is a positive measurement also. Paul says, "Rather, speaking the truth in love, we are to grow up in every way" (Ephesians 4:15). Previously we noted that this could be translated, "truthing in love"—that is, living the truth in love. As we have seen, that means developing an honest and realistic approach to life and to other people—not a brutal frankness but a gracious, loving acceptance of others that always seeks the benefit of others. It is an attitude that lives out the fundamental law of life which Jesus laid down: "Love your neighbor as yourself."

Face the failures

Maturity means a return to realism about yourself. It means to accept yourself as God accepts you: a person with certain unchangeable characteristics which God Himself has given you and which therefore are advantages, no matter how much they may seem like disadvantages to you now. These characteristics include your physical looks, your temperament, your family and ancestry, and your mental endowments. Having all these characteristics, you now learn that as a Christian you are the dearly beloved child of a heavenly Father who patiently teaches you to rely upon the life of His Son. That resurrection life within you is the only resource you need to meet every demand that life can make upon you.

He knows that it's hard for us to learn to rely on Him, and He has made arrangements in advance so that no mistake or failure we make (deliberate or otherwise) will ever in any way diminish His loving concern for us and His fatherly care over us. For our own good, however, He desires that we recognize these failures and sins for what they are and to be realistic (mature) about them, so that we can learn and grow to become more like Christ. He wants us to call our flaws exactly as He calls them—and until we are able to see ourselves as He sees us, we will have difficulty experiencing and realizing His undiminished love for us.

As long as we live in a state of unreality and denial about ourselves, we are susceptible to the lies of the enemy. Only by honestly facing our failures for what they are can we be freed to enjoy the warmth and enrichment of God's fatherly love, and to experience the power to live out the life of the resurrected Lord.

Your progress in maturity can be measured by the degree to which you accept the truth about yourself and others in love. That truth will be both shocking and healing. You will be shocked to learn how strong the human tendency is to preserve attitudes, habits, and behavior which arise (as the Bible says) from the flesh, the old nature. Healing and growth come by understanding that you no longer need to make yourself perfect by your own efforts in order to be accepted and loved by God. You are now free to be yourself, without pretense, without having to hide or defend yourself. You are committed to growth and change, but you no longer feel condemned and ashamed simply because you are not yet perfect. That is an attitude of maturity.

The shock of self-discovery

When missionaries first arrive in a foreign country, they usually experience something called "culture shock." It happens when people find themselves plunged into a totally new situation where all the familiar cues that made them feel at ease are absent. They find themselves unable to communicate with others, and are thus powerless to show others just how intelligent and valuable they are. This is especially true when a new language must be learned, and month after month of study scarcely enables you to carry on a conversation at the marketplace level. It can be a shattering experience.

Among new missionaries, this culture shock often manifests itself in some form of rejection. They reject the country they are in; they cannot stand anything about it, everything is wrong. They criticize and find fault with almost everything. Sometimes the rejection is leveled against the mission board that sent them out. Or they blame fellow missionaries for not properly preparing them before they came. Or they turn this rejection inward and blame themselves, doubting their fitness to serve God on the mission field. Older, wiser missionaries learn to recognize rejection as a symptom of culture shock, and can often help to steady the new missionaries, so that they can get safely through the crisis.

Something much like this takes place with every new Christian as well, a spiritual form of "culture shock." After all, Christianity is a totally different way of living. It relies upon completely different resources and requires quite opposite reactions from those we utilized as "natural" men. It is a form of culture shock to learn that all the familiar props to our ego are taken away from us, and we are confronted with the shock of self-discovery. We learn that much of our acceptance by others was dependent upon impressions and images we project but are not consistent with our inner reality. They were poses, roles we were playing, phantoms of our imaginations.

All the ego-salving techniques which the world commonly employs, and which we once found perfectly acceptable, are now unacceptable as Christians. The "you-scratch-my-back-and-I'll-scratch-yours" attitude which is the basis for the relationships of the world is not the basis for Christian relationships, and is no longer approved. Instead, we must learn to love our enemies and do good to those who despitefully use us. We must pray for those who persecute us—and in our natural selves, we don't want to do that!

The world may be impressed by whether or not we are intelligent, attractive, charming, witty, skilled, or accomplished—but the Holy Spirit is not impressed at all. This produces a "culture shock" in the new

Christian that can be terribly disconcerting and frightening. But once we accept this new and amazing reality of the love of a heavenly Father, we become free to live as God intended us to live when He created the first man and woman. The measure of spiritual freedom we experience from day to day is the measure of our maturity.

Is there anything we can do to spur ourselves on to greater maturity? Is there anything we can do to help others in the body of Christ become more mature? Yes! That is the goal of every pastor, elder, youth leader, Christian education director, and Sunday school teacher! We accelerate our own maturity by developing our spirituality—that is, our spiritual health. The more our spirits are attuned to God and obedient to the Spirit, the better prepared we are to grow and mature in the Lord! Maturity comes by a constant endeavor to live spiritually and obediently.

Paul says this very plainly in 1 Corinthians, where he deals powerfully and insightfully with the issue of Christian maturity. "Yet among the mature we do impart wisdom," he says, "although it is not a wisdom of this age or of the rulers of this age, who are doomed to pass away. But we impart a secret and hidden wisdom of God, which God decreed before the ages for our glorification" (1 Corinthians 2:6–7).

Note that Paul says, first, there are two kinds of wisdom: (1) wisdom of this age and (2) a secret and hidden wisdom of God. He says that the rulers of this age—that is, the wise and important leaders of the world around us—do not understand this secret wisdom of God. They don't understand the processes of the kingdom of God and the ways people react to one another within the kingdom of God. "None of the rulers of this age understood this," he said, "for if they had, they would not have crucified the Lord of glory" (1 Corinthians 2:8).

The mind of Christ

But there is a second kind of wisdom, a wisdom not of this age, a wisdom given by the Spirit—the secret and hidden wisdom of God. Paul then quotes from Isaiah 64:4, saying, " 'What no eye has seen, nor ear heard, nor the heart of man conceived, what God has prepared for those who love him,' God has revealed to us through the Spirit" (1 Corinthians 2:9–10).

The Spirit, therefore, who has given the revelation of truth in the Scriptures, has given us a secret and hidden wisdom designed for our glorification—that is, to lead us to the place where we're ready for glory, a place of spiritual maturity. He goes on to say what this wisdom is: "For the Spirit searches everything, even the depths of God. For what person knows a man's thoughts except the spirit of the man which is in him? So also no one comprehends the thoughts of God except the Spirit of God" (1 Corinthians 2:10–11).

Here is wisdom. The wisdom of this age is the "wisdom" of human thoughts. But the wisdom from above is the true wisdom of God's thoughts. He says, "Now we have received not the spirit of the world"—which is involved with the wisdom of the world—"but the Spirit which is from God, that we might understand the gifts bestowed on us by God. And we impart this in words not taught by human wisdom but taught by the Spirit, interpreting spiritual truths to those who possess the Spirit" (1 Corinthians 2:12–13). These spiritual truths are the secret truths that prepare us for glorification. There is no way we can understand these secret truths apart from the Spirit of God within us, who teaches us these things.

Paul concludes the passage, saying, "The unspiritual man does not receive the gifts of the Spirit of God, for they are folly to him, and he is not able to understand them because they are spiritually discerned. The spiritual man judges all things, but is himself to be judged by no one. 'For who has known the mind of the Lord so as to instruct him?' But we have the mind of Christ" (1 Corinthians 2:14–16). The spiritual man is the man who has learned by the Spirit to think and view life as Christ does. He has the mind of Christ. He has learned to see all the daily circumstances of his life as God sees them, in God's perspective. He is not, therefore, likely to be influenced by natural thinking, a view of things that the world in its unregenerate condition would take.

This is the difference between natural thinking and spiritual thinking. Spiritual thinking marks the mature Christian, the spiritual Christian, while unspiritual thinking marks the immature, or unspiritual, Christian. The immature or unspiritual Christian is still a Christian, but he or she is given to natural thinking—the thinking and "wisdom" of this dying age.

Now what is this secret and hidden wisdom Paul says is imparted for our glorification? Paul describes it clearly in Colossians, at the close of the first chapter, where he is speaking again about maturity. In Colossians 1:26 he says the secret wisdom of God is "the mystery hidden for ages and generations but now made manifest to his saints." To them, he says, speaking especially of the Gentiles, "God chose to make known how great among the Gentiles are the riches of the glory of this mystery [now here it is, here's the mystery], which is Christ in you, the hope of glory."

What is the mystery? The mystery that we are saved by the death of Christ, yet living by His life in us! His life reproduced in us is the mystery that results in maturity and the secret of spirituality. Being spiritual means living on the basis of Christ at work within us.

"Him we proclaim," Paul continues, "warning every man and teaching every man in all wisdom, that we may present every man mature in Christ" (Colossians 1:28). Maturity comes as we grow in understanding this secret of how to live by His life in us. Paul adds, "For this I toil, striving with all the energy which he mightily inspires within me" (Colossians 1:29). That is, Paul's own maturity comes from the secret source of Christ's life at work within him, reproducing His life in the life of Paul. As a result, Paul is empowered by God to teach others, encourage others, and bring others to maturity.

Joined and knit together

We must always keep in mind that we are members of the body of Christ. In the closing lines of Ephesians 4, the apostle Paul puts the issue of maturity into perspective, showing us that maturity is not a purely individual matter. It is a process that takes place within a network of relationships, within the context of "the whole body, joined and knit together by every joint with which it is supplied, when each part is working properly" (Ephesians 4:16).

Paul here says that one of the factors that encourages growth in maturity is to allow other Christians to minister to you. The parts of the body are designed to meet one another's needs—they are joined and knit together. The apostle actually coins a word to express the mutual ministry of members of the body to each other. The word for "joined" is made up of three Greek words: one is the root from which we get our English word *harmony*; another is the word *with*; and the third is the word for *choosing*. The richly complex idea Paul conveys to us by this one compound word is this: God's design for the church is that Christians should relate to one another honestly yet lovingly. As they carry out this mutual "truthing-in-love" ministry, the result will be that choices and decisions will be made with harmony throughout the church. The end result of that church harmony will be that the church will be a witness to the world, and that clear witness will attract people, increase the numbers of the body, and strengthen the body spiritually.

All of this tremendous meaning is embodied in that one three-part word! Of course, this concept is easier said than done! It takes a Spirit-led blend of courage and compassion to speak the truth in love. It takes a willingness to accept others, forgive others, forbear with others, and compromise on *secondary* issues so that our *primary* issues—our unity, our love, and our witness—may *never* be compromised.

The other people in the body of Christ are God's chosen instruments. Do not reject God's instruments! He knows what you need better than you do. You are where you are because that is where God wants you. He put you with the Christians around you because they are the kind you need and you are the kind they need. They may be rather prickly and thorny and hard to live with—and they may think of you in cactus-like terms as well! But they are what you need at the present time, and you are what they need.

So don't struggle with the place in which God has put you. Accept it, welcome it, and seek to relate in honest love to the other Christians around you. As each member of the body accepts his or her role in the body, and seeks to carry out that role, ministering to the rest of the body in truth and love, then the body will grow more healthy. Each member of the body will be doing what he or she was meant to do and equipped to do. As gifts are used and love is expressed throughout the body, a marvelous harmony will emerge—a harmony that leads to maturity throughout the body and produces a witness that will draw thousands more men and women out of their darkness and into the church.

Yes, there will be pain at times. But through the pain will come growth. As you go on, remember that day by day, hour by hour, moment by moment, the Spirit of God is working a miracle. Individual Christians are growing into the maturity of Jesus Christ. The whole body together is manifesting in an increasing way the wholesome, balanced, well-adjusted manhood and stature of Jesus Christ.

Our goal, and the goal of the church, must be the same as that of God, as expressed by Paul in Ephesians 4: The goal is *maturity*.

CHAPTER 12

IMPACT!

Publisher's Note: Pastor Ray Stedman retired as pastor of Peninsula Bible Church in 1990, and went home to be with the Lord on October 7, 1992. Most of this chapter, like the rest of this book, contains Ray's original insights and convictions, carefully edited and updated from the original 1972 edition of *Body Life*. As Dr. Billy Graham observed in his foreword to the original edition, this chapter is where "the author relates how his interpretation of the church has worked effectively in the crucible of practical experience."

For this revised and updated edition of *Body Life*, we have also added new material, drawn from interviews with people at Peninsula Bible Church, both in the pastorate and the laity. These new "Update" sections are separated from Pastor Stedman's words. They offer a perspective on how the *Body Life* principles have found new modes of expression over the years. Our society has changed greatly in the decades from the 1950s to the year 2000—and PBC has changed too! Though the core concepts of *Body Life* are as unchanging as the New Testament itself, there are endless ways in which the exciting vibrancy and vitality of *Body Life* can be expressed. Even though Pastor Stedman is no longer with us, the body life of PBC goes on in ever new and creative ways.

What happens when a church in the twenty-first century chooses to operate on these principles? Will they work today as they did in the early church? The answer is a resounding Yes! Jesus said, "Upon this rock I will build my church; and the gates of hell shall not prevail against it" (Matthew 16:18 KJV). When He said those words, our Lord had all the centuries of future history in view, until His return.

Dr. E. M. Blaiklock, Professor of Classics at Auckland University in New Zealand, has said, "Of all the centuries, the twentieth is most like the first." Today, as in the first century, Christians are a minority group, representing a minority viewpoint in the midst of a hostile, despairing, pagan world. Now as then, Christians are hemmed in on every side by violence, ignorance, immorality, and existential despair. Christians today find themselves thrust back into the very climate where the persecutions and triumphs of the book of Acts occurred.

The Christianity of the book of Acts is not unusual Christianity—it is *typical* Christianity, functioning as it was designed to function. The sterile Christianity of our times is the distortion, with its coldness, its bureaucratic structure, its perfunctory ritual, and its bland conformity. Every century has had its distorted forms of Christianity, but every century has also known something, at least, of the vital transforming power of Jesus Christ at work through His body. That power has been manifested in the present century also, strongly at certain times and places, weakly elsewhere, depending on the degree to which individual churches have discovered and implemented (deliberately or accidentally) the biblical pattern of church life that we have explored in this book.

To manifest life

This would be a good place to summarize that biblical pattern so that we can keep its essential features before us. A church that operates on the New Testament body life model should display these features:

• A pervasive spirit of love and unity, resulting in an attractive, persuasive evangelistic witness to the world (see John 13:35; Ephesians 4:3).

• A celebration of spiritual gifts; all members of the body are encouraged to discover and use their gifts.

• A horizontal rather than vertical "command" church structure; a recognition that Christ alone is the "head" of the church; while the leadership and pastoral gifts are respected and acknowledged, the gifts, creativity, and initiative of *all* the people (the laity) are utilized and *all* members of the body are honored (see 1 Corinthians 12).

• A recognition, drawn from Ephesians 4, that all believers are ministers, not just the pastor-teachers; those with the gift of ruling elder or pastor-teacher are to *build up* and *equip* the entire body of believers to be ministers in the church and in the world.

• An emphasis on scriptural truth rather than human wisdom, social expectations, or religious traditions.

• Frequent opportunities for believers to confess their sins and hurts, to share one another's burdens, to care for one another in *koinonia*-fellowship and agape-love, and to speak the truth in love.

This, in a nutshell, is body life.

And this is a radical departure from the attitudes, priorities, and institutions of this world. Sadly, it is also a radical departure from the agenda and structure of most *churches* in our culture! All too many churches today have more in common with the patterns of this world than with the body life pattern of the New Testament.

We all too easily forget that the church is not on earth to do what other groups can do, but to do what *no* other group of human beings can possibly do. It is designed to manifest the life and power of Jesus Christ in fulfillment of the ministry which was given Him by the Father, as He stated in the synagogue at Nazareth: "The Spirit of the Lord is upon me, to preach good news to the poor. . . . to proclaim release to the captives and recovering of sight to the blind, to set at liberty those who are oppressed, to proclaim the acceptable year of the Lord" (Luke 4:18–19).

The healing ministry of the church is to be carried out through the activity of many, not just a few. It takes the whole body to do the work of the church. Every Christian is endowed with certain gifts which were promised by the resurrected Christ when He ascended on high to the Father's throne and took over the reins of the universe. Our task as members of the body is to discover our gifts and put them to work. If anyone neglects his or her gift, the whole body suffers.

The power by which these gifts operate is reliance upon the imparted life of the indwelling, resurrected

Lord. God has made full provision for every Christian to discover, develop, and use these spiritual gifts in resurrection power through the "shaping up" ministry of apostles, prophets (who lay the foundations of faith), evangelists, and pastor-teachers (who use the Word of God to motivate, cleanse, and strengthen the people for their tasks). As we carry out this biblical pattern, the church will function as salt and light in the midst of a world of corruption and darkness. At the same time, the church will increasingly manifest the wholeness and beauty of the humanity of Jesus Christ.

One church's body life

With considerable reluctance, I now turn to the experience of a single church in order to demonstrate from real life how these principles work in today's world. The church I am qualified to discuss is the one I served as pastor from 1950 to 1990: Peninsula Bible Church, located on the San Francisco peninsula, in Palo Alto, California. There are many churches that could serve to illustrate the principles in this book, but my experience forces me to write only about the church I know best, the church known to its members as PBC.

Is PBC a perfect church? By no means! We've made many mistakes through the years—some merely embarrassing, some absolutely grievous. We are still learners, led by the Holy Spirit into continually unfolding vistas and clearer understanding of the principles we seek to follow. We have learned much from the experience and teaching of others, and feel most keenly our debt to members of the body of Christ in many other churches for their ministry to us. It has been exciting to see the growth and changes at PBC over the years. PBC has been a thrilling adventure in ministry and, I think, a successful experiment that continues to grow and change. Compared with the New Testament standard, of course, we often fall short, but God is gracious and He covers our mistakes with His love. I believe PBC can best be described by the word of Jesus to the church at Philadelphia in Asia Minor: "Behold, I have set before you an open door, which no one is able to shut; I know that you have but little power, and yet you have kept my word and have not denied my name" (Revelation 3:8).

PBC was begun by five businessmen in 1948. These five men and their families felt the need for a warmer time of informal fellowship and Bible study than they were obtaining in the churches they were then attending. They didn't intend to start a new church—just a supplemental experience of close caring and fellowship to add onto their more traditional church experience. They rented a small room in the Palo Alto Community Center and began to hold Sunday evening meetings, while still attending their own churches in the mornings.

Looking back, it's clear that these five families were hungering for the *koinonia*, the body life, of the early church. They achieved this experience to a considerable degree, and the meetings were so enjoyable that they attracted many others who dropped in regularly for the Bible teaching (often by visiting pastors), the songfests, and the inviting, informal atmosphere.

As the group grew, an evening Sunday school class was added, so that children could receive Bible instruction while their parents were in the evening meeting. By the fall of 1950, the number of people attending—both adults and children—was running around a hundred per week. The demands of such a large and fast-growing group became more than the five original leaders could handle in their spare time. It was clear that what had started as a Sunday evening Bible study had somehow become a church! It was clear to everyone involved that God was leading this church to find a shepherd. So, in September 1950, I was privileged to be called as the first full-time pastor of this fledgling church.

Now most of the principles we have explored in this book were either unknown or vaguely understood by me when I first arrived as pastor of what would eventually become Peninsula Bible Church. However, there was one principle discussed in this book that was a clear conviction in my heart, even back then. It was the conviction, derived from Ephesians 4, that the work of the ministry belonged to the people, not to the pastor. I was rather uncertain as to precisely what that ministry was, but I felt right from the beginning that my task as pastor was to unfold the Word of God in its fullness, as best I could understand it, and leave the major ministry responsibilities to the laypeople. Those lay responsibilities included visiting the sick, leading church services, and evangelizing the world— all ministries that were traditionally associated with the role of the pastor!

We determined from the start that we would do no direct evangelizing in the regular services of the church, or within the church building. Instead, our plan was that all evangelization would be done in homes, in backyards, on the campuses, in rented halls, or in other public meeting places.

We didn't feel we were inventing anything new. In fact, we were consciously trying to return to the original blueprint of the church, as found in the New Testament! Amazingly, however, what emerged was a church unlike any church any of us had experienced before!

Koinonia at PBC

The Sunday evening Body Life service at PBC was born as the decade of the violent 1960s faded into history and the more hopeful year of 1970 came into being. At a New Year's Eve service, held till midnight on December 31, 1969, the sharing of the people was so warm and moving that the pastoral staff, meeting the next week, asked themselves, "Why can't we have meetings like this all the time? How can we keep this beautiful spirit of love and mutual ministry going in our church?"

Out of those questions a determination grew to have a service where people could bear one another's burdens and confess their sins and pray for one another as the Scripture commanded. So we made Sunday evenings our regular time for this special experience we called the "Body Life service."

After the Body Life service had been a fixture in our congregation for over a year, I wrote a special column for the May 21, 1971, issue of *Christianity Today*, describing what takes place in a typical Sunday evening Body Life service:

> It happens every Sunday night. Eight hundred or more people pack into a church auditorium designed to seat comfortably only 750. Seventy per cent are under twenty-five, but adults of all ages, even into the eighties,

are mingled with the youth, and people of widely varying cultural backgrounds all sit, sing, and pray together.

A leader stands at the center front, a microphone around his neck. "This is the family," he says. "This is the body of Christ. We need each other. You have spiritual gifts that I need, and I have some that you need. Let's share with each other." When a hand goes up toward the back of the center section a red-haired youth runs down the center aisle with a wireless microphone. It is passed down the pew to the young man, who stands waiting to speak. "Man, I don't know how to start," he says, his shoulder-length hair shining as he turns from side to side. "All I know is that I've tried the sex trip and the drug trip and all the rest but it was strictly nowhere. But last week I made the Jesus trip—or I guess I should say that He found me—and man, what love! I can't get over it. I'm just a new Christian, but man, this is where it's at!" A wave of delight sweeps the auditorium, and everyone claps and smiles as the leader says, "Welcome to the family. What's your name?"

Other hands are waving for recognition. The leader points to a well-groomed, attractive woman in her mid-thirties. "I just wanted to tell you of the Lord's supply to me this week," she says into the mike. She is a divorcee with small children. Her income had dwindled to the point that she'd had only forty-two cents to eat on that week. But unsolicited food had come. The family had eaten plenty, and she wants to share her thanksgiving. Another enthusiastic round of applause.

Then a sensitive-faced girl with waist-long hair: "I just want the family to pray with me. My brother's blowing his mind with LSD, and it's killing me to watch him coming apart, but we can't get him to stop."

"Phil, go over and stand by her and lead us all in prayer for this real need," the leader requests. "You were on LSD, you know how it feels." A tall, thin youth with a scraggly beard crosses to the girl, takes the mike. "O Father," he prays, "you know how Ann feels and you know how her brother feels. Show him the way out, through Jesus, and show him that you love him just the way he is." He goes on, his prayer eloquent in its simple earnestness, the whole audience listening quietly, with bowed heads.

Then a clean-cut college boy is on his feet, his Bible in his hand. "I just want to share something the Lord showed me this week." For five minutes he expounds a verse from the first letter of John, and the crowd laughs with delight at his practical application.

Other needs are shared. One youth asks for prayer that he might be able to buy a car cheaply so he won't have to depend on hitch-hiking to get to his college classes on time. When the prayer is finished, a middle-aged housewife stands at the back and says, "I don't know how this happened, but just this week the Lord gave me a car I don't need. If Ernie wants it, here are the keys."

She holds up a ring of keys, and the crowd applauds joyously as the boy runs to pick up the keys.

Then an offering is announced. The leader explains that all may give as they are able, but if anyone has immediate need he is welcome to take from the plate as much as ten dollars to meet that need. If he needs more than ten, he is warmly invited to come to the church office the next morning and explain the need; more money would be available there. While ushers pass the plate, a young man with a guitar sings a folk song that asks, "Have you seen Jesus my Lord? He's here in plain view. Take a look, open your eyes, we'll show Him to you."

After the song someone calls out a hymn number, and everyone stands to sing it together. Then the teacher for the evening takes over. There is a rustle of turning pages as hundreds of Bibles are opened. For perhaps twenty-five minutes the teacher speaks, pacing the platform, Bible in hand. He illustrates with simple human incidents, some humorous, some sobering. The crowd is with him all the way, looking up references, underlining words, writing in the margins. A few hands are raised with questions on the study. The teacher answers briefly or refers the question to an elder or pastor in the congregation. Then the people stand for a closing prayer. They join hands across the aisles and sing softly, "We are one in the Spirit, we are one in the Lord."

When the meeting is dismissed, few leave. They break up into spontaneous groups, some praying, some talking excitedly about a Bible passage, some singing quietly with a guitar, some just visiting and sharing with one another. Gradually the crowd thins down, but it is a good hour or more before everyone is gone and the lights are turned out.

The gathering is called a Body Life service, a time for members of the body of Christ to fulfill the function of edifying one another in love. It began in January of 1970 when the pastoral staff of Peninsula Bible Church met to discuss the spiritual status of the church. Concern was expressed about the Sunday evening service, which at that time followed a conventional pattern of song service, announcements, Scripture, special music, and preaching. Attendance was rather sparse, running about 150–250 with only a handful of youth present. The major concern was whether we were fulfilling the admonition of Scripture to "bear one another's burden, and so fulfill the law of Christ." Other texts haunted us, such as, "Confess your faults one to another and pray for one another that you may be healed, [admonish] one another in psalms and hymns and spiritual songs." Where was this occurring among our people? Where could it occur?

We determined to make a place for this ministry by wiping out the traditional structure of the evening service and using the time to invite a sharing of needs and gifts by the people. We began with the question, "Where are you hurting? Not where did you hurt ten years ago, but now, where are you right now?"

Predictably, it was slow getting started, but soon a climate of honest realism began to prevail. When that was noised abroad, without any particular invitation youth began to appear—many long-haired, barefoot, and

in bizarre dress. Our middle-class saints gulped at first
but were determined to be genuinely Christian. They
welcomed the young people, listened to them, prayed
with them, and opened their hearts. The kids did
likewise.

The numbers increased by leaps and bounds. For
over a year now it has been going on with no sign of a let-
up. Every service is different. Love, joy, and a sense of
acceptance prevail so strongly that awed visitors
frequently remark about a spiritual atmosphere they can
almost scoop up in their hands. *Koinonia* has come![1]

The Jesus movement of the tie-dyed, flower-power
'60s and '70s is gone now, and many of the features
that characterized body life at PBC have changed with
the times. In fact, the Sunday evening Body Life
service is no longer held at PBC—but genuine body
life goes on. Peninsula Bible Church continues to be
committed to the principles of ministry found in
Ephesians 4. Many other churches across the country
and around the world demonstrate body life in their
own way, through their own forms of expression, in
the midst of their own unique regional and cultural
 context. Whenever a church is ready to take
Ephesians 4, 1 Corinthians 12, and Romans 12
seriously, the Lord of the church is ready to heal and
to bless.

Update:
In recent years, people have come to Peninsula
Bible Church for the first time as a result of reading a
prior edition of *Body Life*. They often ask, "When is the
Body Life service?" And they look stunned and
disappointed when they hear, "We don't have Body
Life services anymore." It's easy to understand why

people might mistake the lack of a Body Life service for a lack of body life—but the fact is that body life is alive and well at PBC!

Body Life services were only one expression of New Testament body life, as lived out at PBC. But true body life—the caring, vulnerable, accepting, forgiving, life-together experience that is celebrated in this book—has always been a pervasive part of every corner, nook, and cranny of Peninsula Bible Church.

"The Body Life service was a phenomenon of the '70s and '80s," recalls one pastor at PBC. "The leadership changed, and the gifts of the new leaders were different than before. Also, the society and the needs of our congregation and community changed. Finally, we realized that it was time to make a change. We couldn't allow the fact that there was a book out there called *Body Life* to keep us from doing what is best for our church ministry. This church has always placed current needs and effective ministry over tradition—even a wonderful tradition like the Body Life service."

People are often surprised today to learn that Peninsula Bible Church is not one but *two* churches. Over the years, PBC has planted a number of churches, but in 1985, a decision was made to divide PBC into two distinct congregations—not one church with two locations, but two completely independent churches, *both* operating on the Ephesians 4 principles of equipping the laity and living in close, caring, *koinonia*-community with one another. The original church in Palo Alto is the "north church," and it serves a community that is largely a mix of older people and Stanford University students. The "south church" is located in Cupertino, at the heart of Silicon Valley, and serves a largely thirty-something community of high-tech engineers and professionals with families.

Dividing into two churches was a ministry decision, not a "church split." PBC has never wanted to be a megachurch, believing that a supermassive size can often work against the sense of intimate body life the church wanted to foster. A large size is also unwieldy in a horizontal structure with widespread lay involvement; a megachurch tends to need top-down, "control"-oriented leadership in order to manage its many far-flung departments and ministries. Deliberately keeping PBC from growing too large has enabled the church to continue focusing on discipleship, the expression of gifts in the laity, and training people to leave and start new ministries rather than focusing on ever-more-ambitious building programs.

Music at both churches remains an eclectic mix of praise songs and choruses, traditional hymns with deep theological content, and contemporary and classical choral works. The focus is on congregational involvement. The rock and folk-rock music of the '70s was attractive to the flower children of the times, but it was essentially concert music, and the congregation tended to be spectators rather than participants.

Today, there is a strong emphasis in both churches on involving the *entire* congregation in all phases of worship, including the ministry of music. While many churches may legitimately choose to offer different styles of music in different services in order to draw in different "audiences"—one service for the Silent Generation, one for Baby Boomers, one for Generation X—PBC maintains a long tradition of uniting rather than segmenting the congregation. The goal of body life is to blend all believers, all groups and sub-groups, into a single body—and the wide range of music employed at PBC is used to support this tradition and draw everyone together in a shared experience of worship.

Body life continues to find new expressions at both churches today. Since it comes straight from the New Testament, body life is an elastic concept, stretching across societal and generational changes. Caring and sharing functions of the original Body Life evening service have been incorporated into aspects of the morning worship service: a monthly body life sharing time, plus a weekly needs-sharing section in the bulletin—a place where people can seek prayer or practical help if they need work or housing, in-home assistance, financial assistance, transportation, and so forth. Caring, sharing, confession, and holding each other accountable also takes place in the many Bible studies, recovery groups, and other small groups in the church.

The original goal of the Body Life service was to charge up and stimulate the body of Christ to live and minister effectively throughout the week. Christians are to be loving, caring, thoughtful servants of others—not merely at a Body Life service once a week, but at all times, wherever they are. That is still the goal of PBC today, and the spirit of Body Life continues to be practiced throughout the week in the communities served by PBC-Palo Alto and PBC-Cupertino.

Is the Body Life service gone forever? Maybe—or maybe not! American culture today shows many of the same features as American culture in the '60s, '70s, and '80s: political and cultural polarization, generational conflict (Generation X versus the Baby

Boomers), distrust of government and other institutions, deep environmental concerns, rising drug abuse, widespread longing for community and healing, and so forth. Could it be that Body Life services, which flourished in the days of the flower children, might actually come back—revived and revised—in the days of Generation X? God alone knows.

A church of small groups

PBC began with a small group, and small groups have been a prominent feature of our ministry since the beginning. Typical of our early small groups were the Home Bible Classes. The primary goal of Home Bible Classes was not to teach Christians, but to attract non-Christians and interest them in the themes of the Bible and in spiritual truth. These groups were deliberately low-key and non-threatening in approach. There was a total absence of activities with a "churchy" flavor, such as hymn-singing, opening prayer, chairs lined up in rows, or a speaker standing behind a lectern. Each group had a host and hostess who opened their home to friends and guests, giving the class the welcoming feel of a purely social occasion. A lay teacher taught from the Bible, seeking to capture the biblical concepts and express them in contemporary terms. Discussion was invited—free-wheeling and no holds barred. Anyone was free to challenge what was presented if they cared to, and their challenges were listened to carefully and courteously. An answer was sought from the Scriptures themselves.

These meetings were an instant success and became so popular that the discussion would sometimes involve scores and even hundreds of people (we had some very large homes available!) and would often continue until the wee hours of the morning. No mention was ever made of PBC at these home meetings, for they were regarded as the personal ministry of the Christians involved. There were soon many new converts coming from these classes, who were then urged to become active in a local church, preferably one close to them. Thus the whole body of Christ in our area began to profit from these classes, and many of the new converts naturally ended up at PBC.

Another "group experience" at PBC that employed many of the same principles as the Home Bible Classes was the young adults group called the Career Class. Since this group often numbered 300 to 400 strong, it could hardly be called a "small group"—yet it truly was "small," intimate, and "non-churchy" in the way it operated. It was, in many ways, a church within a church—but this was a church for mostly single adults. It met in a restaurant every Sunday morning, using the teaching gifts not only of Pastor Ron Ritchie, but of a large staff of lay teachers. There was a significant dynamic of *koinonia* in the Career Class, of needs being met, of people being vulnerable and available to one another, of disillusioned, broken, and searching people finding their way into a caring, loving, supportive family. Many young adults have found their way to Christ by walking through the doors of that restaurant.

These group experiences—the Home Bible Classes and the Career Class—accomplished three important ends: (1) They were an effective tool for reaching unchurched "worldlings" right where they were (in neighborhood homes and in a restaurant—not a church building), and to introduce them personally and directly to the Lord of glory who had come into the world to call the lost, and not the righteous, to repentance. (2) They were a visible demonstration to our Christian people that the gospel still has power to transform lives, and that the gospel could be tremendously attractive to non-Christians when presented without all the religious trappings of a church service. (3) These classes gave many Christians an opportunity to become personal channels of God's Spirit at work, and showed them what an exciting adventure it can be to discover and use one's spiritual gifts in a group setting. Gradually, the turned-on spark of exciting, vital Christianity began to spread throughout the congregation at large.

These group ministries helped to overcome what we came to call "the huddle syndrome"—the tendency of Christians to huddle together, avoiding anything but the most superficial contact with worldlings, avoiding close friendships or extensive hospitality with non-Christians. If we lose contact with worldlings, we lose our ability to influence and reach them with the transforming gospel of Jesus Christ. In the Home Bible Classes and Career Class, Christians recovered their confidence in the power of the gospel and they lost their fear of the world. Instead of relying on a programmed approach to evangelizing, we found that witnessing and evangelizing was being done, powerfully and effectively, through personal friendship and hospitality.

Update:
The emphasis of PBC continues to be *relationships over program*, and the people of PBC recognize that

relationships are best developed and strengthened in smaller, more intimate settings. Small groups are also used as a place where laypeople can discover and use their own spiritual gifts, while observing and affirming each other's gifts. For example, one of PBC's men's groups went to Eastern Europe as a short-term mission project, and many of these men discovered ministry gifts they never knew they had—and one even became a full-time missionary to Romania!

PBC's small groups are under the Care Ministry umbrella, and consist of:

• **Men's Growth Groups,** small groups for men who desire to grow together in Christ in an atmosphere of honesty, accountability, and mutual encouragement.

• **Women's Growth Groups,** small groups for women who desire support and encouragement in applying God's truth to the issues of women in today's changing society.

• **Special Needs Groups,** small groups focused on specific needs and issues, including recovery from sexual abuse, recovery from co-dependency, twelve-step recovery from substance abuse.

All of these groups have a strong evangelistic dimension, since they are aimed at attracting non-Christians and getting them involved with believers in applying the Scriptures to everyday problems.

The Career Class, which met for many years in a local restaurant, has a counterpart in today's PBC as the Twenty-something group, which holds midweek meetings in homes. Twenty-something continues to attract young career-age people, many of whom go on to become involved in either the Palo Alto or Cupertino church.

The Care Ministry also offers seminars, Bible studies, Search for Significance groups, and other groups and services for people who are hurting, needing help, or just desiring to grow in their faith. The purity of body life, of distilled New Testament Christianity, finds endless and varied modes of expression. The vulnerability, caring, and sharing of the large Body Life services of the '70s has largely moved into smaller, more intimate contexts of small groups. This is a reflection of where we are as a culture—and of where PBC is as a congregation.

Campus and youth ministry

Being strategically located near Stanford University, Peninsula Bible Church has always had a strong commitment to an Ephesians 4 ministry within the college community. One of the first associate pastors of our church, David Roper, spearheaded our church's witnessing efforts at the university—an effort which became, in my judgment and to my knowledge, the most effective on any campus in the world. It was Christian young people who stood on the front lines at the campus, boldly and enthusiastically sharing their faith with their peers, doing the work of the ministry that God gave the church to do.

We also applied the body life principles of Ephesians 4 ministry to high school ministry. The addition of Ron Ritchie to our pastoral staff in 1969—which corresponded with the upsurge of the West Coast "Jesus movement"—gave us an opportunity to see literally hundreds of high school students baptized as new converts to Jesus Christ. So vital was their Christian commitment that they moved out in ministry and bold witnessing throughout their community, and far beyond. It is exciting to see many of these same young people return to PBC, and to see that their faith has remained stable as they matured, and that they now serve God as pastors and laypeople in churches across the country and around the world.

We have used these same Ephesians 4 principles of ministry with Christians of all ages and all backgrounds, even with children. We have found that junior high and even junior age children are capable of discovering and exercising their spiritual gifts, and of learning how to rely on resurrection power to effectively serve God. As a consequence, we have seen our junior high young people helping to teach younger children with great effect. And in the summers, we have sent teams of youngsters out under adult leadership, holding weeklong meetings for children in remote towns and villages of California, Oregon, and Nevada. Beside the fruit this ministry bears in the lives of many spiritually neglected children in these little towns, our own Christian young people have been powerfully impacted by seeing that God is able to use them in ministry, even though they are young. Since the young people themselves did all the planning and conducting of the meetings, they were able to learn—by their own experience!—the great lessons of trusting the faithfulness of God.

Update:

Since the 1970s, the pressures and perils of being young in America have only increased. Drugs are as prevalent today as in the '70s, and many of those drugs—such as crack cocaine—are more addictive and more deadly than ever before. Today's entertainment media are more explicitly anti-God and sex-drenched than ever before, influencing our young people toward rebellion, immorality, and self-destructive behavior at an alarming rate. Our schools no longer tell our children, "Be moral." Instead, they say, "Be careful," and thrust a condom in the child's hand. Children today fear nuclear war, terrorism, environmental destruction, social collapse, and AIDS. Most young people today come from what used to be a cultural rarity, what we once called "a broken home" (when was the last time you heard that term?). Divorce rates and teen suicide rates are at an all-time high.

Clearly, there is a greater need now than ever before to reach young people with the gospel and bring them into a caring community where they can share their pain and fears, where they can find love and acceptance, and where they can be trained and discipled to take part in a cause that is larger than themselves—the cause of Christ. Ministry to children and youth at both PBC churches continues to follow the Ephesians 4 plan. The kids themselves do the ministry.

For example, young people from both churches engage in mission ventures to Mexico and in the local community. They plan the trips and the events themselves. Adults are there to give guidance and answer questions, but keep hands off as much as possible, so that the young people themselves can totally own the ministry. In these settings, the young people of PBC discover their own gifts and ministry skills, and they learn to rely on themselves and each other to provide leadership rather than relying on some vertical authority to tell them what to do and how to do it. These lessons will last a lifetime and carry Peninsula Bible Church far into the future.

Internship and training programs

The endless creativity of the Holy Spirit has produced approaches and innovations which, in our human wisdom, we could have never planned or expected at PBC. An example of this is the intern training program at PBC, called the Discovery Center. This grew out of the concern of the pastoral staff to do something to meet the need for practical ministry for seminary students during summers. The academic pressures and climate of seminary made it difficult for young ministerial students to put to work some of the principles they were learning, so PBC undertook to bring one or two young men each summer to work with the staff in outreach ministry.

Many of these students were found lacking in three major areas of scriptural understanding: the spiritual walk of an individual in reliance on resurrection power; the understanding of spiritual gifts and how the body of Christ functions; and the position and power of the church in relationship to society and social problems. Summer after summer these concepts were taught to young seminarians, with PBC bearing the expense of their ministry, involving a monthly salary of $250 for single students, and $300 per month for married students. The number varied from two to a maximum of twelve in any given summer.

Then young people began coming to us and saying, "We've heard of your training program and we want to get in on it. We will come for a year or so, and pay our own expenses, if you will let us join this program." We discouraged this at first, feeling it would put too much strain upon the pastoral staff, but several were so persistent that we made a venture and took two young people on for one year. When word of this got out we were flooded with applicants, and finally were forced either to make provision for this influx or abandon the effort entirely. We went ahead, trusting God to lead, and thus began our internship program.

Out of this program evolved the Scribe School. Scribes were chosen from lay applicants in all age groups and from varied backgrounds. It was a kind of informal seminary for laypeople with a desire to understand and teach the Scriptures. For two years, they were plunged into the Greek and Hebrew languages, guided in the discovery of practical teaching skills, and introduced to matters of theology and church history. Each scribe maintained a close association with individual pastors in a tutorial capacity. Scribes, unlike interns, worked at regular jobs to maintain their own support.

Update:

The Scribe School no longer exists in the same way it once did. Its functions have been folded into the Discovery Center internship program, which continues in both churches to this day. The Discovery Center holds quarterly sessions for interns and anyone else who wishes to attend. The internship program changes focus and emphasis over time, but is consistent in its commitment to on-the-job ministry training for laypeople and seminarians. The two PBC churches are never without interns.

Pastor Stedman always believed that the church ought to equip all the saints for ministry—the children, the teenagers, the college students, the laity, and the seminarians. It is not the pastors who are on the front lines of ministry; it is the people—all the saints—whose job it is to go out into the world, to land on the beachheads of the world, to take the territory, to win the world by the quietly transforming resurrection power of Jesus Christ.

Discovery Publications

Still another development that was never planned or promoted but grew from small beginnings is that of Discovery Publications (which, by the way, is not connected with Discovery House Publishers of Grand Rapids, Michigan). This publishing arm of PBC began with the interest of a young graduate student in geology at Stanford, Peter Irish, who found his eyes opened to fundamental spiritual realities through a series of sermons preached on Ephesians 6, entitled "Spiritual Warfare." He determined to make these messages available in printed form for the benefit of others, and on his own he organized a group of volunteers to transcribe tapes of the messages, edit them, type them on stencils, and run off mimeographed copies. These proved so popular he was encouraged to treat other sermon series in the same manner. He eventually found it necessary to devote his full time to this work.

The messages were advertised by word of mouth, and a large mailing list was gradually built up. Soon, copies of these messages were going out across the country and around the world. Today, these messages are offset printed and include a catalog of messages in stock that cover large areas of the Scriptures, as well as many topical studies of great practical importance, such as studies on sex, marriage, family relationships, parenting, the occult, social issues, and so forth. Even though the two churches, Palo Alto and Cupertino, are completely independent, Discovery Publications serves both churches, providing tapes and transcripts from both pulpits to a vast worldwide mailing list.

This, then, is the state of Body Life at Peninsula Bible Church today. Who are the ministers at PBC? The people of PBC! What is our job as pastors? To equip the saints "for the work of ministry, for building up of the body of Christ"! (Ephesians 4:12). In the shadow of the ivy-clad walls of Stanford University, and in the fast-paced, high-tech world of Silicon Valley, this is what Peninsula Bible Church continues to believe and stand for today.

This, I am convinced, is what the church must stand for, with a sense of urgency and passion and boldness, as a new millennium begins.

BODY LIFE

Problems and Solutions

Over the years, I've encountered a number of questions regarding the principles in this book. As I have met pastors and concerned laypeople from place to place, they have often asked how these biblical concepts might be put into practice in a local church, under varying conditions. Typical questions and the answers we have found through experience at PBC are given below in order to help you to put these principles into effective practice in your church.

Q. "In a church that has for years followed a more conventional approach, where should a pastor begin to implement these concepts?"

A. The proper place to begin is with an exposition of the Scriptures from the pulpit, over a period of time. Expositional preaching will help the church see that the Bible does teach these principles, and that they have behind them the weight of biblical authority. The pastor must be gracious and loving, not lashing out at his people, but gently leading them to the place where they will be ready and enthusiastic to embrace these changes.

Q. "What can be done by laypeople when a pastor resists these scriptural principles and refuses to consider them?"

A. This is a delicate situation, though unfortunately it is met all too frequently. Perhaps a church board can send its pastor to a conference where these principles are taught, or ask him to meet with other pastors who have experienced these concepts at work; or perhaps a copy of this book may help him. A thoughtful and patient approach will usually work wonders in this type of a situation.

Q. "If these principles are so clearly taught in Scripture, why wasn't I taught them in seminary?"

A. That is a difficult question to answer. It is easy for a seminary to begin to train men to fit what the churches are looking for, rather than to hold closely to the biblical pattern. Tradition is a powerful force, and seminaries, like individuals, can succumb to the pressure to conform. In the course of church history, it is the seminaries that are reformed by the spiritual awakenings among the churches, rather than vice versa. Many seminaries, however, are moving strongly toward a renewed emphasis on these biblical principles.

Q. "I agree that what you've presented is scriptural, but it demands tremendous motivation to get a congregation moving in this direction. How do you supply this motivation?"

A. Motivation can come from three sources: an awareness of the desperate condition of the church today; the hungering of individuals after excitement and challenge in ministry; and the conviction, arising from the Scriptures, that God will act as He has said. Try a bit of all three.

Q. "How would you recommend that we start a Body Life service?"

A. First, do not try to borrow a few techniques of leadership and expect the service to go. A Body Life service must emerge from the deep conviction of a congregation that they have a responsibility before the Lord to "bear one another's burdens." They must be helped to see the need for sharing, for honesty, and for mutual acceptance. When they respond to these with conviction, then it is time to try a Body Life service. Keep the service as simple as possible, and above all, don't over-organize or attempt to manipulate it. Also, be aware that many of the features of an effective Body Life service—authentic caring, vulnerability, accountability, acceptance, confession, and forgiveness—can be performed in the intimate setting of a small group or home Bible study.

Q. "Aren't you afraid that exhibitionists will take advantage of such a service to relate scandalous matters?"

A. Despite the openness of Body Life services at PBC, nothing like this has occurred. If it did, the leadership would welcome it as an opportunity to teach the congregation appropriate ways to share about certain kinds of problems. The individual involved can also be invited to meet with a pastor or elder afterward. If this is done graciously, it will turn an embarrassing moment into a tremendous congregational learning experience.

Q. "Isn't it unwise to share your innermost secrets with others? Isn't it better to keep them entirely to oneself?"

A. No, it is not better to keep them to yourself! Christians are explicitly instructed in Scripture to bear one another's burdens, and we are equipped, through various spiritual gifts, to do so. Of course, some selectivity should be observed as to the trustworthiness of those with whom one shares, and certainly deep dark secrets should not be aired publicly, but no Christian should have to struggle on alone, wrestling with some terrible habit or overwhelming situation. He is cheating himself of the help of the rest of the body if he does not share with someone.

Q. "What spiritual gifts should I have to be a pastor?"

A. Of course you should have the gift of a pastor-teacher. This is fundamental. It is manifested by compassion toward those in need, and an ability to teach the Scriptures in such a way as to see people delivered by truth. Other gifts are helpful, such as gifts of wisdom and knowledge, discernment, prophecy, showing mercy, and the gift of faith.

Q. "Should all our Sunday school teachers have the gift of teaching?"

A. By all means! Sunday school teachers should not be selected because they are willing or because no one else will do it. They should show some ability to improve the spiritual life of others through teaching before they are entrusted with a class. Molding the lives of young people through teaching is far too important to trust it to the unqualified.

Q. "What if a congregation is so small that it does not have qualified teachers for the Sunday school?"

A. Then it would be much better to have the children taught at home by their parents. Also, the Scripture instructs a church to "pray therefore the Lord of the harvest to send out laborers into his harvest" (Matthew 9:38). We have filled many a vacancy in our Sunday School by this method.

Q. "Is it wrong to give an invitation in a church service?"

A. It is not a question of being wrong but rather of being inappropriate. There are occasions when it is most appropriate, if done graciously and sincerely, without undue emotional appeal. But in general it tends to weaken a church to make this a continual practice, for time must then be taken from the work of equipping the saints unto the work of the ministry. There is very little time available for this anyhow in the usual church service, and that is surely a far more important matter when the makeup of the congregation is essentially Christian.

Q. "How long will it take to get a congregation operating on Ephesians 4 principles?"

A. That depends entirely on the individual congregation and its pastor or pastors. It will probably take much longer than one would at first think, for Christians often require much thought and time before they accept new approaches. But if only a few in a congregation catch on and start exercising their spiritual gifts in resurrection power, it will be a spark that will ignite others and gradually pronounced change can occur. Remember, "The Lord's servant must not be quarrelsome but kindly to every one, an apt teacher, forbearing, correcting his opponents with gentleness" (2 Timothy 2:24).

Q. "Is there any word of encouragement you can say to a pastor who is just beginning to put Body Life principles to work?"

A. Yes. Here it is, from 1 Peter 5:2–4—"Tend the flock of God that is your charge, not by constraint but willingly, not for shameful gain but eagerly, not as domineering over those in your charge but being examples to the flock. And when the chief Shepherd is manifested you will obtain the unfading crown of glory."

STUDY GUIDE

QUESTIONS FOR INDIVIDUAL AND GROUP STUDY

Publisher's Note: These questions have been designed to help you apply the principles of *Body Life* to your own life and church situation. They are designed to make this material more meaningful either in your own private study or in a small group study, such as a Sunday school or home Bible study group.

The questions are divided into three sections. The first section, *See Your Own Reflection*, is designed to help you "break the ice" and begin to identify with the issues being explored in the chapter. The second section, *Dig a Little Deeper*, is designed to help you wrestle with the specific biblical and practical issues of the body life principles. The final section, *Let's Get Personal*, is intended to help you apply body life principles to real-life situations in a personal, practical way.

We wish to express a special word of appreciation to Mr. Charles Luce, who prepared an initial and extremely valuable draft of this Study Guide. We hope this study enriches your understanding of these concepts and enables you to experience the exciting adventure of Body Life!

Chapter 1

The Most Powerful Force on Earth

See Your Own Reflection:

1. Pastor Stedman observes that not only is every church a mixture of true and false believers, but every believer has within him or her a mixture of true and false character and behavior.

Look back over this past week. When did you show signs of true Christian character and behavior? When did you show signs of false character and behavior?

Dig a Little Deeper:

2. What are the three major contributions that the church has made in every generation for good, for light, and for moral restraint?

Identify the ways in which your church is demonstrating those contributions.

3. Read Matthew 13:24–30 and Matthew 13:36–43. What does the wheat stand for in this text? What do the weeds (tares) represent?

Describe the difference between the true and false believers. Why does God say not to separate them in your church?

What has happened when a church has attempted to separate them?

4. Pastor Stedman observes that God has designed the church to be a kind of invisible government, influencing and moving the visible governments of the earth. Study Matthew 5:13–14, Philippians 2:14–15, and 1 Timothy 2:1–2, then consider:

What would be the influence of this "invisible government" on the visible governments of the earth?

What does this concept teach us about our responsibilities as citizens?

Let's Get Personal:

5. Does your church demonstrate Christian character? If not, why not?

What specific aspects or actions of your church do you base your assessment on?

If not, what do you personally plan to do to help your church become more scripturally Christian, as God intended it to be?

Memory Exercise: Matthew 13:43.

Chapter 2

The Church's Highest Priority

See Your Own Reflection:

1. How do you define and set priorities in your own home or business?

What is God's highest priority for the church? Why do you believe God has set this priority for His church?

Dig a Little Deeper:

2. Compare the first-century society of the New Testament with the society you live in. What similarities do you see? How does this comparison help you to apply the truths of Scripture to your life and your church?

3. Read 2 Corinthians 4:18 and John 19:10–11. How do Jesus and Paul illustrate the attitude that God wants to develop in Christians today?

4. What is God's strategy for relieving human darkness and misery in the world?

How does God's strategy differ from the strategy of the world's systems?

5. In the opening chapters of Ephesians, Paul gives clear statements regarding the nature and purpose of the church.

What does Paul mean when he says that we have been destined to be adopted as God's children? For what purpose are we appointed? (See Ephesians 1.)

What does it mean that Christians are no longer strangers or sojourners? (See Ephesians 2:11–19.)

What is the *holy mystery* of the church? (See Ephesians 3.)

Let's Get Personal:

6. How does your life demonstrate the life of Christ? If it doesn't, explain why not.

What do you plan to do to demonstrate the life of Christ in a more effective and consistent way?

As you make these changes in your own life, what effect do you think these changes would have on the spiritual health of your church? Can one person make a difference?

If you are studying this book in a group, ask the group (or someone in the group) to hold you accountable regarding the changes you intend to make in your life.

Memory Exercise: Ephesians 4:1–3.

Chapter 3

Not Union—Unity

See Your Own Reflection:

1. Was the home you came from essentially intact or essentially broken? If you came from a broken home, how did that experience affect you?

How do you think God is affected when His family is "broken" by strife and disunity? How are others in the church affected? How are people outside the church affected?

Dig a Little Deeper:

2. Why does Paul exhort Christians to unite? (See John 17:17–21.)

What is God's part in producing oneness in the Christ?

What is the Christian's part?

What causes friction among Christians?

Are there ever times when it is justifiable for Christians to fight among themselves? Explain.

3. Read 1 Corinthians 3. What is the source of division in this passage?

What are some other sources of church division and disharmony that you have heard of or seen? What would it take to heal that division?

4. Explain what faith is. Why is Paul able to say that there is only one faith, and that faith is in Jesus Christ?

5. What is the one true baptism? (See 1 Corinthians 12:12–13.)

How is it different from water baptism?

6. Describe a situation where you met someone who was very different from you in some way (culturally, regionally, economically, politically, or even doctrinally), yet in whom you saw the same living Lord who lives in you?

What did you feel? How did you respond? How did the other person respond?

Let's Get Personal:

7. Read Jesus' prayer in John 17:20–26, the prayer for all believers He prayed just before going to the cross. Explain why that passage gives rise to the phrase "Our oneness is our witness."

What are you consciously doing in your life, your neighborhood, or your career to demonstrate the unity of the Spirit, so that people around you will see the life of Jesus in you?

What could you do to demonstrate the unity of the Spirit so that you would be a more effective witness to those around you? If you are in a group, ask someone to hold you accountable this week to be a living witness of the reconciling love of Jesus.

Memory Exercise: Ephesians 4:4–6.

Chapter 4

All God's Children Have Gifts

See Your Own Reflection:

1. What was the best gift you ever received as a child? Why was it so special? How did it make you feel?

Now, magnify that gift by a hundred times, and imagine that God Himself has given you this magnificent, wonderful gift—a spiritual gift, a grace of the Holy Spirit. How does that gift make you feel? What would you like to say to God or do for God in response?

Dig a Little Deeper:

2. Who in the church body should be expected to reach the unsaved?

3. Read Ephesians 4:7. What are two things God has given Christians for their work in ministry?

4. Describe what the words *grace* and *gift* mean. How do you think that these characteristics equip us for ministry?

5. Examine Romans 12:6–8, 1 Corinthians 12:4–11, and 1 Peter 4:10–11. List all the spiritual gifts that are indicated in those passages.

Let's Get Personal:

6. What gift or gifts do you feel the Holy Spirit has given you?

If you are doing this study in a group, select a person you know well, whose life you have observed. What spiritual gift from this list do you see in him or her?

Memory Exercise: Ephesians 4:7 or 1 Corinthians 12:4–6.

Chapter 5

Discovering and Using Your Gift

See Your Own Reflection:

1. How many different work situations or service situations have you had since you finished school?

In which of these situations did you feel most comfortable and confident? Why?

In which did you feel out of your depth and overwhelmed? Why?

Dig a Little Deeper:

2. What is the difference between spiritual gifts and natural gifts (abilities and talents)?

3. Can natural gifts contribute to your effectiveness in the exercise of your spiritual gifts? If so, how?

4. How do you discover spiritual gifts?

5. Explain why the diversity of gifts eliminates all need for competition within the body of Christ.

Let's Get Personal:
6. Name one spiritual gift you are currently using. How did you discover you had that gift?

How has the exercise of your spiritual gifts enhanced your own life and your faith?

Select someone in your group and affirm the ways in which that person's gifts have contributed to your life or the life of the church.

Memory Exercise: 1 Corinthians 12:14, 26–27.

Chapter 6

According to the Power

See Your Own Reflection:

1. How did the power of Jesus' resurrection become real to you? Was it a slow, gradual realization—or a sudden, overwhelming transformation of belief?

Dig a Little Deeper:

2. What is the fundamental secret of how the church is to function?

3. What is the inexpressible gift that has been given to every Christian?

4. Why can't we effectively use our gifts without Christ?

5. Describe resurrection power. What is it like? How does it work? Why do Christians need it? How do we know we have it?

Let's Get Personal:

6. Pastor Stedman used the illustration of appliances using the same electrical power to energize them to perform their various functions. Identify a number of effective Christians in your church carrying out different functions: What kind of "appliance" is each of these Christians?

What kind of "appliance" are you?

How have you seen Jesus Christ supply you with the energizing power you need to minister in your church?

Memory Exercise: Philippians 3:10.

Chapter 7

How the Body Works

See Your Own Reflection:

1. At what time in your life has your own physical body been in tip-top condition? What factors contributed to your bodily health?

When has your body been in its worst shape? What factors contributed to your poor state of health?

Dig a Little Deeper:

2. Read Ephesians 4:11–12. What lessons are there in the physical body that we can apply to the body of believers, the church?

3. What was the role of the original apostles?

What, if any, is the role of an apostle in the church today?

4. Describe the gift of the prophet.

What, if any, is the role of a prophet in the church today?

5. Read 1 Corinthians 14:32 and Peter 1:19. Why are we to pay attention to what the apostles and prophets teach?

6. Describe the role of an evangelist. Are all Christians called to evangelize? If so, what does it mean to have the spiritual gift of an evangelist?

As Christians seeking to reach the world for Christ, what should our message be?

7. Describe the role of pastor-teacher.

8. Describe the role of elder. What is the difference between a ruling and a non-ruling elder?

Is a ruling elder a ruler or a servant? Explain the biblical reason for your answer.

9. Consider the ministry, programs, and "family life" of your church. Do you feel your church is built upon human programs designed to meet God's purpose? Or is it built on programs initiated by Christ to fulfill His purpose for the church? Does it or does it not function as God intended? Explain your answer with specific examples.

Let's Get Personal:

10. Compare the organization and structure of your church with the organization and structure of the early first-century church. How does your church differ from the biblical plan? How is it the same?

Memory Exercise: Mark 10:42–43.

Chapter 8
Shaping Up the Saints

See Your Own Reflection:

1. Looking back over your life, who is the one person who has done the most to mend, equip, prepare, and shape you up for ministry?

How did that person affect your life? Give examples.

Dig a Little Deeper:

2. Explain what is meant by expository teaching and preaching of God's Word.

Why is it the most effective way of preparing the saints for their work of ministry?

3. What is the required attitude for one to speak the Word of God? Why is this true?

4. What is the biblical balance between evangelism and pastor-teaching of the body?

5. What happens when each member of the body is not fully engaged in the work of the ministry?

6. Compare the role of elder in the early church with the role of elder in your church today.

Compare the role of pastor-teacher in the early church with the role of pastor-teacher in your church today.

7. What is to be the attitude of the pastor-teacher in his role of training and preparing the saints for ministry?

8. Take another look at the chart in chapter 8 on page 115. Where do you find yourself and your role on that chart?

How well are you performing your role?

Why do you think God has organized the church this way?

9. Are the four "equipping-roles" functioning in your church? Why or why not?

What additional training or equipping do you desire to be better equipped to minister?

Let's Get Personal:

10. Is your prayer life effective in enabling you to perform your role, as illustrated in the above chart?

If you are studying this book in a group, how can the other members of your group support you, pray for you, encourage you, and hold you accountable to effectively carry out your role in the church?

Memory Exercise: Ephesians 4:11–12.

Chapter 9

The Work of the Ministry

See Your Own Reflection:

1. When you consider "the work of the ministry" that God has called you to, do you feel:
- Fearful?
- Eager?
- Confused?
- Confident?
- Inadequate?
- Ashamed?
- None of the above?

Explain your answer.

Dig a Little Deeper:

2. Read Luke 4:17–21. What is the work that Jesus was given to do?

3. Since Jesus has returned to the Father, whom has He left behind to carry on His work?

4. Read John 14:12. What are the "greater works" that will be done? Who will do them?

5. There are five divisions of Jesus' work that the church is to carry on. Describe each of them.

6. What is the most important lesson you have learned from this chapter?

Let's Get Personal:

7. Consider for a moment the gifts God has given you. How are you using them to carry on the work of the ministry God has given the church?

Is there an area of ministry that you have never tried that would be a good use of your gifts? What prevents you from getting involved in that ministry?

Memory Exercise: Luke 4:17–21.

Chapter 10
Keeping the Body Healthy

See Your Own Reflection:

1. What do you do to keep your body healthy?

What do you do to keep yourself spiritually healthy?

What do you do to maintain the health of the body of Christ, the church?

Dig a Little Deeper:

2. What is required to build up the body of Christ into a healthy church?

3. What are the spiritual diseases that cause individuals to become spiritually unhealthy?

That cause churches to become spiritually unhealthy?

4. Pastor Stedman suggests small group gatherings as a way to help build unity in the church. Do you have small groups in your church? Are you in such a group?

If so, how could these groups be improved and strengthened to further the health of the entire body?

5. What does it mean to speak the truth in love?

What would it mean to speak the truth without love? Give examples. What would the result be of speaking the truth without love?

What would it mean to love without being truthful? Give examples. What would the result be of love without truthfulness?

6. What prevents Christians from being open and vulnerable?

How can we help each other overcome the fear of exposure to that keeps us from opening up to one another?

7. List some practical, specific ways we can show love for one another in the body of Christ.

Let's Get Personal:

8. Without naming names or breaking a confidence, describe a time when you had to speak the truth in love by offering correction or a loving rebuke to another person. Was it a difficult experience or a joyful experience?

In light of such passages as Galatians 6:1, Ephesians 4:15, Philippians 2:8, and 1 Peter 5:5, do you feel you did a good job of speaking the truth in love?

Describe a time when someone confronted or corrected you. How did it feel? Do you believe that person's motives were pure, or that he/she was trying to "nail" you in an un-Christlike spirit? How could that person have handled the situation better? How could you have handled it better?

Memory Exercise: James 5:16.

Chapter 11

The Goal Is Maturity

See Your Own Reflection:

1. Among all the people you know, whom would you say is the most mature?

What is the one quality that, in your mind, marks that person as mature?

Are you consciously trying to reproduce that quality of maturity in your own life? If so, what specifically are you doing about it?

Dig a Little Deeper:

2. What is the Lord's goal for us as Christians, according to Ephesians 4:13–16?

3. How does the Bible define the concept of Christian maturity?

4. According to Genesis 1:26–27, we were made in the image of God. Now, according to Ephesians 4:15 (compare Romans 8:29), God wants us to be re-made in the image of Jesus Christ. If we were already made in God's image, why do we need to be re-made in the image of His Son?

Why doesn't God simply produce Christlikeness in us at the moment of conversion?

How is Christlikeness produced in us?

5. What must be known about a Christian before he or she is placed in a position of responsibility or leadership in the church?

6. How does God look at you in this growth process? Is He a slave-master, lashing a whip at your back? A stern teacher standing over your shoulder, glaring at all the mistakes you are making? Or a cheerleader, spurring you on to greater effort and achievement?

How do your fellow Christians view your growth? Are they slave-masters, stern teachers, or cheerleaders?

How do you view your own growth? Are you slave-master, stern teacher, or cheerleader for yourself and your own progress?

Let's Get Personal:

7. Sometimes spiritual growth is painful, sometimes pleasant. Describe a painful situation in your life that helped you to become more like Christ.

Describe a pleasant situation in your life that helped you to become more like Christ.

Which have you found to be a more effective means of producing maturity—pleasant circumstance or painful circumstances? Why?

Memory Exercise: Ephesians 4:13–16.

Chapter 12
Impact!

See Your Own Reflection:

1. In your own words—and, if possible, from your own experience—sum up what the term *body life* means to you.

Dig a Little Deeper:

2. Many people consider America to be a "Christian nation." Why, then, does Pastor Stedman call Christians "a minority group, representing a minority viewpoint in the midst of a hostile, despairing, pagan world"?

As a Christian, do you see yourself as part of a "minority group"?

3. Pastor Stedman lists a number of features of New Testament body life. On a scale of 1 to 10, how would you rate your church in the following features:

• A pervasive spirit of love and unity.

• A celebration of spiritual gifts.

• A horizontal rather than vertical "command" structure.

• A recognition, drawn from Ephesians 4, that all believers are ministers, not just the pastor-teachers.

• An emphasis on scriptural truth rather than human wisdom, social expectations, or religious traditions.

• Frequent opportunities for believers to confess their sins and hurts, to share one another's burdens, to care for one another in *koinonia*-fellowship and agape-love, and to speak the truth in love.

4. What specific actions would you like to see your church take in order that it become more like the New Testament body life pattern?

5. What specific actions are you willing to undertake—giving of your own time, resources, skills, and spiritual gifts—in order to help your church conform to the New Testament body life pattern?

Ask someone to hold you accountable to take these steps or make these changes in your life.

Let's Get Personal:

6. Pastor Stedman warns against "the huddle syndrome"—what he calls "the tendency of Christians to huddle together, avoiding anything but the most superficial contact with worldlings, avoiding close friendships or extensive hospitality with non-Christians." Do you have non-Christian friends, and are you having an influence on those friends for Jesus Christ?

If not, what could you do to start having more contact with "worldlings"?

How could others (for example, friends in your small group) help to hold you accountable to make changes in your life so that you would have a greater impact on the "worldlings" in your neighborhood and your workplace?

Memory Exercise: Ephesians 5:25–27.

NOTES

Chapter 2: *The Church's Highest Priority*

[1]Will Durant, *The Story of Civilization*, Part III, "Caesar and Christ" (New York: Simon and Schuster, 1944), p. 566.

[2]Edward Gibbon, *The Decline and Fall of the Roman Empire*, Vol. 1 (New York: The Modern Library, Random House), p. 382.

Chapter 3: *Not Union—Unity!*

[1]Lucy Maud Montgomery, *Anne of the Island* (New York: Bantam Books [reissue edition], 1992), p. 83.

[2]Bernard Ramm, "The Continental Divide in Contemporary Theology," *Christianity Today* (October 8, 1965).

Chapter 10: *Keeping the Body Healthy*

[1]Quoted by John R. W. Stott in *One People: Laymen & Clergy in God's Church* (Downer's Grove Ill.: InterVarsity Press), p. 88.

Chapter 12: *Impact!*

[1]Ray C. Stedman, "The Minister's Workshop," *Christianity Today* (May 21, 1971).

Note to the Reader

The publisher invites you to share your response to the message of this book by writing Discovery House Publishers, P. O. Box 3566, Grand Rapids, MI 49501, U.S.A. For information about other Discovery House books and music, contact us at the same address or call 1-800-653-8333.